FAREWELL TO FEAR

FAREWELL TO FEAR

Nelson L. Price

BROADMAN PRESS
NASHVILLE, TENNESSEE

Dewey Decimal Classification: 152.4
Subject heading: FEAR
Library of Congress Catalog Card Number: 83-15242
Printed in the United States of America

Dedication

Contents

1
The Force of Fear

The city was under siege. As when a house is on fire, the inhabitants wanted to flee. The populace seemed eager to save themselves, even if naked and ashamed. Others heard of the calamity and received the exiles. Tales of the horrors which had befallen the city were widespread; stories of tortured souls shook the city. Shaking of foundations was a well-known cause of alarm.

Now every heart quivered. All saw death daily before their eyes. Terror was constant. Many were shut up within the walls of their own houses. The enemy was encamped around. Without charges there were those who roamed the streets seeking the guilty as well as the innocent. Formerly free persons sat shackled, anxiously inquiring of those they felt safe to ask, "Who today has been seized, carried off, or punished? How did it happen? How did they fall?" The people lived a life more dreadful than death.

This calamity is an enigma, isn't it? In this scene there is flight without an enemy. Inhabitants are expelled without a battle. There is captivity without capture. No fires of barbarians are visible. No faces of the enemy are seen. Yet, all suffer as those carried into exile. They tremble for their own

11

safety. They are no better off than the dead. They are already dead—*with fear.*

The city is your town. That is the world in which we live. A stark terror that rules by day and night is the emotion of fear. Whether real or imagined, the result of the cleated boot called "fear" is the same. It is the suppressive. Those subject to its siege who are defeated are that—defeated. Though they walk the streets without visible restraints, they are captive. Even while exercising freedom of speech, they endure cowardice. Fear whips, defeats, cowers, and humiliates the financially rich, as well as the poor; the physically strong, as well as the weak; the charmingly beautiful, as well as the uncomely and unattractive. Both young and old are subject to its influence. Fear has no racial bias. Its hollow laughter can be heard ringing through the corridors where it has been unleashed.

We are urged to live "without fear." The Greek word for fear is *phobos.* When it appears with "a" before it the translation is often "without fear"—or actually "fearless." The Old English use of "less" means minus. The encouragement then is to act *minus fear.*

This is wise because fear puts us into a "still-frame" phase of life. Most persons have watched a film where there is plenty of action. Suddenly, the action has frozen. The producer has chosen to remain on one scene. It has become a "motion picture" no longer but the "still-frame" effect has stopped action.

Fear freeze (or still) frames us, causing us to stop creative and productive action. One who is afraid to act, doesn't act; so, stagnation results.

No emotion so completely robs the mind of all its powers

of reason and action as fear. Fear, being an apprehension of pain, operates in a manner that resembles actual pain.

If physical pain results from the movement of a particular muscle, we don't use that muscle as freely, if at all. Whether that pain is real or imagined, the result is the same—limited or no use of the muscle. The same is true regarding fear of any real or imagined mishap that might cause pain. Whether the pain is real or imagined, the influence is just as strong in either instance. It may take the form of physical, psychological, mental, emotional, financial, or sociological pain. When one fears something or someone, he is apprehensive of pain. This causes limited or no action as an avoidance tactic. *Fear immobilizes.*

A basic difference between fear and pain is obvious. Pain most often operates on the mind by way of the body. Fear generally affects the bodily organs by the operation of the mind which suggests the danger. Each, primarily or secondarily, produces tension, contradiction, or emotional response of the nerves.

The person who does not master a fear is a runaway. The conditions and circumstances with which life has matched us are our challenges. If in fear we cower away from them, the very challenge intended to afford us opportunity masters us by cowardice. We run away.

The Source Against Fear

"Fear not," counseled *HE*. Who is *He? He* must know the strength of my fear. *He* must be aware of the effect of my apprehension. The weight of my worry must be known by *him*. My anxiety does not overwhelm *him*.

His "fear not" must mean *he* knows more than I, loves stronger than I, and is more capable of dealing with the source of my fear than I.

"Fear not" is an unequivocal statement. Thus, the resources *he* is willing to make available to me, in order to deal with my fear, must be greater than my fear. This implies there is a resource more than sufficient for my need. I am encouraged to know that helpful assistance is available to me.

He is the Source. He is the Source able to help. He is the Source willing to help. He is the Source wanting to help. I am not able, though willing and wanting help; I am not adequate to handle my fear alone. I need the Source. Pronouns for him abound. Most persons feel comfortable with those used in the Bible. Whatever pseudonym is used for him, he is the Lord God of eternity. The Almighty speaks of his strength as superior to all others. The "Ancient of Days" declares his durability. He has overcome and outlasted all factors involved in fear.

The applied title "Source," not being found directly in the Bible, may appear strange. The Psalmist alluded to it when he sang, "My help cometh from the Lord." The Lord is the Source of help. James indicated it when he wrote, "Every good gift and ever perfect gift is from above, and cometh down from the Father of lights" (James 1:17). Paul was obviously aware of God as the Source when he penned this refreshing fact, "My God shall supply all your need according to his riches in glory by Christ Jesus" (Phil. 4:19). There is a name for God which enables me to comprehend a bit more about him. *Jesus* is his stage name. This does not infer he was play acting, but rather represents this earth as a stage on which the drama of life is played out by us. God, with an epidermis, was and is called Jesus Christ. In human form he kept reiterating "fear not."

That makes me all the more hopeful. Not only has he observed our scene, but humankind has seen how he dealt with and spoke about the horrors which frighten us. As man, Jesus never once used his supernatural powers for his own welfare. He was as much man as though he were not God and as much God as though he were not man. This is a miracle which I don't understand but I can comfortably accept. As the God/man—man/God, he taught us much about how to deal with fear. By practice and precept he taught. Gradually a significant segment of the cowering society with which he dealt caught on. The combustibility of who he was and what he taught has resulted in a world-wide flame which still burns in the hearts of millions. He is the Source of our resource for dealing with fear. Without him you and I have every right to fear.

A Power Stronger Than Fear

For a moment let us step behind the scene and observe him as Creator. As the Source of all that exists, he is greater than all. A basic law of science reveals that the cause must always be equal to or superior to the effect.

The next time you are afraid during the day, step outside and look up. Even if it is cloudy there is light. He declared, "Let there be light: and there was light" (Gen. 1:4). "God made two great lights; the greater light to rule the day . . . " (Gen. 1:16a). We call this sphere, this greater light, the sun. To produce its light the sun consumes 4.2 tons of its substance every second, every second throwing off into space more energy than man has used since civilization began! Only about one two-billionths of that energy reaches the earth. The sun contains about as much mass as 330,000 earths. Its volume is about 1,300,000 times that of earth. Even though it is being consumed at a rate of over four tons per second, there is enough of it to last for another five million years.

How does it make such light? Long before Albert Einstein penned his famous equation, $E = mc^2$, the Source set nuclear fusion to work. Deep within the interior of the sun, temperatures are approximately 16 million degrees Centigrade (25 million Fahrenheit), and pressure is a trillion pounds per square inch. It has been calculated that a pinhead of matter at the temperature of the sun's core would emit enough heat to kill a person a hundred miles away.

The light that illumines our days spreads from the sun's surface to planet Earth at the rate of 186,000 miles per second and reaches here in about 8½ minutes.

When you begin to think about the enormity of the cause of our fears, pause and reflect on this. He who created the sun with a spoken word, "Let there be light," also said, "Fear not." The same power and authority are behind both statements. Look up. Relax!

"And the lesser light to rule the night: he made the stars also" (Gen. 1:16b). Therefore, if you walk outdoors at night, note the sky. It can enable your spirit to soar.

Our home is located on the crest of Georgia's beautiful Pine Mountain in Cobb County. The elevation makes the night sky clearer. In the autumn it is a joy to walk out on our deck and search the sky for Pegasus, a constellation of the Northern Celestial Hemisphere. Try it. Once you have found it, look for a pale bit of light near the upper left-hand corner of the Great Square of Pegasus. That is the spiral galaxy of Andromeda. It is larger than our Milky Way. It is one of one hundred million galaxies. It is two and a half million light years away. It consists of one hundred billion suns many of them larger than our own sun!

Look at it. Think about it.

Now consider your size and your problems. Ask yourself, "Is the God who made that big enough to help me with my problem?"

Fear causes us to lose our perspective. Of course, this God of the universe is bigger than the cause of our fear. But when we focus on our fear and forget him, the relativity is lost. An inordinate preoccupation with fear distorts reality. It is smart to back off and evaluate what is happening as unemotionally as possible. Feed your mind on fear-defensive facts. Let your mind bask in the magnificence and might of God. Readjust your perspective.

Fear is like a runaway horse. Once the panic begins, there is little control. Logic affords firm pull on the reigns. Think! Employ your gift of reason.

Arturo Toscanini, the stellar conductor, always sought perfection. He also had a way of putting the situation into perspective. He incited good musicians to excellence. Dynamically, he always drove them and himself with urgent intensity. On one occasion, while conducting Beethoven's "Ninth Symphony," everything went note perfect. Upon completion, the excited musicians exchanged glances as if to say, "Even Maestro Toscanini must be pleased." The audience offered the ultimate of compliments of that day by sitting completely silent in tribute.

With his arms slightly raised Toscanini stayed at the podium. Courteously, he leaned forward and whispered to the orchestra, but was overheard by the audience as he asked, "Who am I? Who are you? Toscanini is nothing. You are nothing. Beethoven is everything."

Toscanini knew that the one who composes is really the one in charge. He and his musicians were merely in concert with the source, Beethoven. Had they violated the musical score, the production would have been ruined. By complying with the guidelines, near perfection was attained. The enormity of the role played by the absent Beethoven was an awareness of Toscanini. The composer's composition had been complied with, and the role of the orchestra was rewarding.

We often become so preoccupied with the sound of our piccolo personalities that we forget our God, the Source. So engrossed are we in sounds and sights most directly affecting us that we forget the reliability of the One who orchestrates the symphony, "Fear not."

Beethoven's music has stood the test of time and now judges its critics. His music is a standard criteria by which musical excellence is determined. What one says about Beethoven's music says more about that person than it does Beethoven's music. Our responses to God's exhortation say more about us than it does Him. He is faithful. He who has promised will bring it to pass. If God says there is no cause to fear, there is none. We who are fearful are by our actions saying, "God, I don't believe you." Or, "God I don't believe you are reliable." Such statements evidence we have failed to realize, "I am nothing. You are nothing. He is everything."

The Path Toward Conquering Fear

A visit to Mount Palomar Observatory gives opportunity to look through telescopes that reveal our galaxy to consist of as many as one hundred billion stars. There are millions of other galaxies as large or larger. Many of these are about one million light years apart. (A light year is approximately six trillion miles.)

Somewhere in trying to comprehend the enormity of all this, our most capable minds run out of reasoning. David must have thought about this when he penned these pertinent words: "Before the mountains were brought forth, or ever thou hadst formed the earth and the world, even from everlasting to evelasting, thou art God . . . For a thousand years in thy sight are but as yesterday when it is past, and as a watch in the night" (Ps. 90:2,4).

The Hebrew phrase translated "everlasting to everlasting" actually means: From vanishing point past to vanishing point future, God always has been and always will be. Think back in time and out into space as far as you can. Now project into the future and out into distant space as far as possible. Somewhere the greatest of thinkers reaches an extremity. That is one's mental vanishing point. Even beyond that God always was, is, and shall be. He is bigger than space and beyond time.

That is the God who has said, "Fear not."

Yet, he is most personal. This big God is personal. Wisely wrote the psalmist (147:3,4), "He healeth the broken in heart, and bindeth up their wounds. He telleth the number of the stars; he calleth them all by their names."

Only a God with an inventory of the universe is big enough to handle our problems. Don't forget, however, he *is* big enough to handle them.

He is a personal, "in-charge" God. He even knows the names of *all* the stars. Humankind with its collective genius has not been able to accomplish this as yet. Our God is one of the acquaintance. He has not lost touch with the remotes of his creation.

Let your heart sing with the ancient musician, "I will say of the Lord, He is my refuge and my fortress: my God; in him will I trust" (Ps. 91:2). As though antiphonally God answers, "Because he hath set his love upon me, therefore will I deliver him: I will set him on high, because he hath known my name" (Ps. 91:14).

Summarily, God commanded, "Fear not."

This God of the vast outer space is vitally concerned about an inner place—your heart. He wants to be your fortress.

Deep in the Arabian desert is a small fortress. It stands silently on the vast expanse of the ageless desert. Thomas Edward Lawrence, known as "Lawrence of Arabia," often used it. Though unpretentious it was most sufficient. Its primary commendation was its security. When under attack, often by superior forces, Lawrence could retreat there. Then the resources of the fortress became his. The food and water stored there were life supporting. The strength of the fortification became the strength of its occupants. When Lawrence defended it, it defended him. As one relying on the garrison, he was the object of its protection. Its strength was his. Old desert dwellers living around there have told me that Sir Lawrence felt confident and secure within its walls. He had on occasion to depend on the fort; It provided his need. He learned to trust it; his experience proved its worth. Like that fort, "The Lord is good, a strong hold in the day of trouble; and he knoweth them that trust in him" (Nah. 1:7).

Like a sparkling diamond atop a treasure trove of jewels, a refreshing truth jumps out of that statement: "He knoweth them that trust in him." Don't ever forget "he knoweth" you.

Often in speaking of celebrities, my daughters would ask me, "Does he know you?" The question was not, "Do you know him?" It was as though I took on importance not by saying I know them, but that they knew me. I am renewed daily by knowing God. I am twice blessed by his knowing me. We, the creatures, take on a new vitality by virtue of being known by him. It is not merely that he knows about us like we know about the ocean. He is acquainted with us. He who knows our downsittings and our uprisings has spoken, "Fear not."

He knows our person, presence, problem, perplexity, pressure, and predicament. And knowing all of this, God of origin says, "Fear not."

He is a caring God who knows of the need of his people, and he can be expected to be an involved God. He who has been likened to a father was spoken of by his uniquely begotten Son, His only-one-of-a-kind Son, Jesus, " . . . what man is there of you, whom if his son ask bread, will he give a stone? Or if he ask a fish, will he give him a serpent?" (Matt. 7:9-10). Our loving Heavenly Father gives no less good gifts to those who ask of him in trust.

Trust and fear not!

A God who can count the stars might be considered big but remote. A truth taught by Christ makes him intimately personal. "Are not two sparrows sold for a farthing [about four cents]? and one of them shall not fall on the ground without your Father. But the very hairs of your head are all numbered. Fear ye not therefore, ye are of more value than many sparrows" (Matt. 10:29-31).

He knows you. He even knows the number of hairs on your head. And if you're bald, he knows the number of dead hair follicles! That is not merely the number of hairs on your head, but he knows your intimate needs and his eternal resources. The Apostle Paul rejoiced to assure his readers, "But my God shall supply all your need according to his riches in glory by Christ Jesus" (Phil. 4:10). That statement included the emphatic "shall." Trust him and it will amaze you how fast your fear flees. Trust in belief strong enough to act.

Time for Triumph

Give him time.

Often we pray for his help and, not getting it as immediately as we anticipate, feel he was not listening or doesn't care. Sure, he is able but does he care? Yes, he cares!

My wife Trudy asked me to grow some spinach for salads. She asked me on a Saturday in early September. Within minutes, because of my love for her and a desire to please her, I tore myself away from the game of the week and went outside to start digging. Within hours I had the soil ready. Before dark the seeds were in the ground and watered. A few days later little green sprouts emerged. Soon tender vegetation was ready for picking. Between the request and the harvest, several weeks passed.

Without knowing the process involved, my wife could have complained that I didn't care, didn't know how to, or didn't want to grow the spinach she had requested. The fact was that within minutes of the request I ambitiously started the process which resulted in providing an answer to her request. During all that time she could have been discouraged and disappointed. She wasn't. She trusted me. After all, one of my collegiate majors was horticulture. Time was required—she knew that. Patiently, she waited on me and the process of production.

Often we make a request of our loving Heavenly Father. Without an immediate answer we temperamentally start complaining. Many times he instantly starts the process necessary to provide our need. Time is required to answer certain requests. Wait on the Lord. Patience admirably displays trust. Upon making the desire known to him, thank him for the process he is beginning in that instance and for the result to come. That is faith.

One elemental aspect of prayer needs to be noted. Our prayers are, after all, requests. They are not mandates or dictatorial demands which the Lord must obey. If a prayer request is turned down, consider who does it? He is One who loves stronger than you and knows more than you. Based on his intense love and superior judgment, he often says no to our requests. No is always a legitimate answer to a request. When he says no, thank him that his love and knowledge, both of which exceed yours, prevailed and he in mercy spared you of your folly.

Let God be God. Give him room and time to act.

While waiting, "Fear not."

He wants to bless you more than you want him to. He is the "good Lord." Don't forget that. He is good. He can't be any other way. It is his inherent nature. It is the nature of water to be wet, of fire to be hot. They can't be any other way. God is good. He can't be any other way. It is his inherent nature. Circumstances and conditions may not be good, but God is. He is. He is always. He always is. Therefore, interpret his involvement in your life in light of his very nature. He is good.

Many confuse what is happening with who he is. Don't!

He is good even when times are bad. That fact can reinforce your mind. It can garrison your spirit. It can defend you from improper attitudes that lead to distrust and fear. Such fear springs from our being apprehensive that God doesn't care or that you don't count. He does and you do. He wouldn't keep up with the hairs on your head if he were not concerned with what is going on in that head.

Faith—The Victory

The Lord who is our stronghold is good. He is, therefore, a good stronghold. Trust him. Have faith. "Fear not."

The desert fortification was available and there were times Sir Lawrence needed it. It would have been of no value unless trusted and used. Our God is a formidable fortification. We need him, often urgently. Sir Lawrence would've been foolish if he hadn't used the resource of the sanctuary's stronghold. Its use often required time and trust. Within it, all of its assets were his. Even if near it and not in it, none of its values were his. Such nearness could have built a false sense of security and overconfidence. It had to be fully used to be of full value.

Don't presume on God's goodness by almost having faith in him—a union of dependence. Then, "Fear not!"

The trust with which we lean upon the bruised reed of human nature is the same as that with which we can lean upon the steel girder of God's goodness. We make the choice. The choice determines the dividends.

All the blossoms and flowers of your life may seem to be victim of life's untimely frost. Their beautiful leaves may now appear curled to death. They will come again. God restores souls. Spring returns. The season of renewal always follows even the foulest winter. No fear is so dreadful and hopeless but that happiness and hope can visit the heart once again, where trust and love abide.

Trust the Lord and fear not. Then your soul will no longer be like "the sea that cannot rest," full of turbulent wishes and passionate desires that come to nothing. Faithless attitudes are full of moaning like the homeless ocean which ever works on the beach, yet produces only yeasty foam, broken shells, and driftwood. The faithful heart becomes translucent and still, like a land-locked lake, where no winds rage or tempests trouble. On its calm surface can be mirrored the clear shining of the unclouded blue. Reflected therein can be seen the Son that never goes down.

Mount Olivet looked down on Jerusalem before Melchisedek was its king. Tabor and Hermon stand watch over the Land of Promise as they did before human lips had named them. They only hint at the durability and endurance of the God who deserves our trust. "From everlasting to everlasting" he is—God. No problem has ever outlasted him. No need has ever transcended his existence. So let him be God—that is, your Boss. He has earned and does deserve the right to be in charge of your affairs. Trust him—fear not.

As residents of New Orleans, our family lived through several hurricanes. When forecasts projected the approach of these destructive freaks of nature, we always secured items. Lawn furniture was brought in, windows boarded up, and food stored. Any items that could not be brought in were tied to a secure mooring. When the winds, which often exceeded 100 miles an hour, swept through the community, many homes were destroyed. All loose items were blown away and destroyed. Many objects tied down with strong ropes were torn up, along with the items to which they were tied. That which kept an item safe was not the rope, but the mooring. Strength and safety were dependent on the anchor.

We, too, must fasten ourselves with the sufficient cords of faith to the Lord Jesus Christ. The storms of life are sure to come. They are inevitable. The Master is a sure mooring.

Even those who trust him most have only begun to trust him as he deserves. We are like tiny music boxes engaged in their narrow round of existence. They repeat over and over their same limited tune. All around them there is a vast sea of music. None of it is pegged out on the music box's cylinder. The music box goes on in its repetitious rounds, playing its own one song. The vast reservoir of musical genius goes unplayed, though it does exist.

We are likewise bound in our extent of trust. We trust with the equivalent of one little ditty while the overtures of grace intended for our lives remain mute. Let the music of your life come out by faith. Let the strings of your slumbering spirit be stirred by the suffering, strife, or suppression; but let them sound forth with music that dispels fear. There is within each of us an even better song of fidelity than has ever come from our lips. Don't be locked in mechanically to your limited trust. Burst forth with a song of praise. Fear cannot survive in such an environment. Sing a new song— the new song of trust.

Our big God is concerned about little things. After all, he put this universe together out of little things. An atom is so small that twenty-five trillion of them could lie side by side in an inch.

Merely consider the hydrogen atom. It contains one

proton with a positive electric charge and one electron with a negative electric charge. A scale model helps us to see the wonder of the minute world involved in such an atom. Let the proton be represented by a ten-inch ball at the center of a circle ten miles in diameter. On the circumference of the circle, the electron is a small marble whirling at the speed of 1,350 miles per second. The God who took such infinite care in structuring the intricate atom cares about little things in your life.

Someone once asked, "Do you think we should just pray about the big things in life?" Another answered coolly, "Do you think there is anything in your life important enough to God to be considered big." Our bigness might be considered little when compared to God, but to him it is big enough to be important. Anything big enough to be of concern to you is not too small for him. He cares about little things. His delicate and diversified atoms prove that. You are more unique than the atom and of far more importance. The atom shall someday be destroyed in a gargantuan cataclysmic climax, but you are eternal. The issues facing you are not, but you are. Remember who you are, and don't concentrate quite as much on what you are facing.

Control Central Is Staffed

He who spoke the atom into existence and set the earth in its orb said, "Fear not."

He is so loving that if he were not in control of things, he would tell us the truth. He is so knowledgeable that if he were not in control, he would know. Because of his love and knowledge, if he were not in control, he would frankly tell us, "You ought to be scared to death." Panic should prevail without his control. That is exactly what does exist in many lives and that is the reason why. He is able to control, but yields control to anyone who protests his mastery. Anyone who refuses his control or willfully remains ignorant of his control legitimately lives in a panic state. When you know who is in control there is no fear.

Robert Louis Stevenson delighted in the story of a ship tossed in a storm. The sea was rough and the rocky coast perilous. Danger was real and dread expectancy active among the seamen. One frantic sailor who was laboring below the water line could contain himself no longer. He rushed to the control room, closed the door behind himself, and stood frozen in fright watching the captain wrestle with the controls of the huge ship. Skill of mind and strength of hand enabled the captain to guide the vessel through the threatening rocks into open water. The Captain turned slightly, looked at the frightened sailor, and smiled. The youth returned below deck and assured the crew all danger was over. When they inquired how he knew, he answered, "I have seen the face of the Captain, and he smiled at me."

If you will only "Turn your eyes upon Jesus, look full in his wonderful face," "the things of earth will grow strangely dim in the light of his glory and grace."

God isn't dead. He isn't even anemic! As a matter of fact, he is smiling.

Trust him. Don't rush him. Wait on the Lord. Be patient. Fear not.

A French surgeon once advised a young intern in the frenzy of a delicate operation, "Don't be in a hurry, for there is no time to lose."

Trust God. Then there is reason to "fear not."

From the archives of my mind this verse recently emerged as I looked out my study window and saw a little bird enact it.

> *Be like the bird in flight*
> *Pausing on boughs too slight,*
> *Feeling them give way, yet sings*
> *Knowing that it hath wings.*

Be bird-like in temperament. Let Jesus Christ be your wings when boughs give way and fright threatens. Trust him. He will bear you up.

2
The Fact of Fear

The answer to humanity's gloom, pessimism, and depression is embodied in the incarnation of Jesus Christ. The act of God becoming man is his way of relating to our troubles and fears. It says, "I am with you always." So stop being afraid. Christ enables us virtually to laugh away our fears in the sunlight of his power and love.

"Fear not," the words on the angel's lips at Christ's birth, were some of his favorites. He did not borrow them from the angels—he lent them to those heavenly messengers on their earthly mission. We are met at every dark corner of life with his cheery, "Fear not!" Those words should be our watchword on our journey and in our warfare. Every time the disciples were worried, anxious, or afraid they heard with joy Jesus exhorting them, "Fear not!" When they fell at his feet trembling, they heard his reassuring, "Fear not!" In their storm-tossed ship they happily heard him cry out "Fear not!" When they shivered, as frightened sheep soon to be scattered without a shepherd, his stabilizing voice urged, "Fear not, little flock." On the occasion of his exodus from this life, he exulted, "Let not your heart be troubled, neither let it be afraid."

Today his "fear nots" can untie your fear knots.

Admit it. You have had—and do have—fear knots. They may have shown themselves as a painful kink in your intestines. Perhaps they have shown up as red splotches on your neck. Sometimes they seem to tie a knot in your esophagus and you refer to them as a lump in your throat. You might even have reacted to fear with a bodily tremble. Whatever form these knots take, they do reveal themselves in all of us. They are discomforting. As unpleasant as they are, many persons seem content to live with them, or are at best unaware that they do not have to live with them.

Fear knots have even been proven forensically to cause responses in the cardiovascular muscles that result in heart failure. Persons thus affected have literally been "scared to death."

These knots are bodily evidences that what goes on in our brains actually affects us physically. There is a plus side to this. If what goes on in the brain is positive, pleasant, and productive, the body reacts in a constructive manner.

Fears that fester are known as *phobias*. Phobias in humans correspond to objects or events we are biologically conditioned to fear. Research into the nature and anatomy of fear was initiated in the early 1920s by the behaviorist psychologist, John B. Watson. His experimentation produced a profile of fear as an emotion, as a motivating force, and as on acquired drive. By modern standards, though, his experiment might be considered ingenious, though I would classify it as cruel. Watson and a collaborating student "conditioned" a one-month-old child to experience intense fear at the sight of a white rat.

The child, still known to psychologists as "Little Albert," was the son of a wet nurse in a Baltimore children's home. "Little Albert" was observed to be a composed infant. He had never been known to be in a state of fear or rage. Temperamentally he was classified as cheerful. The experiment involved exposing him to a series of stimuli which could have frightened him—a white rat, a rabbit, a dog, a monkey, and masks with and without hair. The baby was delighted and responded affectionately to each. He appeared to enjoy contact with the animals but most especially with the white rat.

In separate tests, Watson exposed the child to a sudden, loud, clanging noise produced by banging two steel bars together. This loud, unexpected noise was a "startle stimulus." It was noted to be fear-evoking by the researchers. "Little Albert" would rear back violently, pause in his breathing, fling his arms up in a self-protecting gesture, and burst into a hard cry.

Soon after this, the scientist began a series of "Pavlovian" condition trials. He presented the white rat and the sudden frightening noise simultaneously. In the first two sessions Watson clanged the two bars together. Each time the child reached out to touch the rat. After only two such times the child would fall forward and begin to whimper. A week later the rat was introduced again. Albert refused to touch it. He had already established a distinctly negative emotional response.

In only seven sessions Albert established an association between "fearful noise" and the "white rat." A short time later the white rat alone produced the same fearful response. Even without the initial, fear-soliciting noise, the rat was sufficient by itself to cause fear. Each time the rat was produced, Albert would cry and crawl away as fast as possible. Further tests five days later revealed that the conditioned, emotional reaction to the white rat had generalized to all "furry" stimuli. He was now afraid of the dog, the rabbit, a Santa Claus mask with white wool on it, and even a sealskin coat.

This test indicated that a child in his natural environment learns to associate a variety of formerly "neutral" stimuli with alarm-evoking or pain-producing events.

This, in part, explains why many inherently harmless things or events might be feared by youth and adults. Though the thing feared might be without any capacity to cause harm or pose danger, it might be linked to something that did. Finding the link might be difficult. Once it is found, breaking it can often more easily be done.

Pause for a moment and evaluate your prime fear. Is it dangerous? If not, with what might you associate it?

A study conducted in the early 1940s by Professor Neal Miller, then of Yale University, shows the force of fear. The intent was to measure the relative strengths of fear and that of the primary drive of hunger. Miller began with some albino rats which had been trained to run down an alley to their food. Later, hungry and restrained by a harness, they pulled toward the food with the strength of 50 grams. Other rats trained to avoid an electric shock at the end of that same alley would pull against the restraining harness with the force of 200 grams. Animals trained to receive an electric shock after getting their food soon refused to return for food, even though very hungry. These and other experiments show that fear interferes with eating and drinking, in spite of hunger and thirst, and with sexual behavior.

In a classic paper that has become a landmark in the experimental study of fear, Professor Miller has demonstrated that the emotion of fear is more than merely a reaction to pain or alarming stimuli. As an acquired drive, it is as powerful as the primary drives of hunger, thirst, and sex.

The effect of these principles is seen on our society in general. The degree of fear we feel about a potentially harmful event may not be linked primarily to the degree of danger or to the amount of injury, but to the quality of the event itself. Some types of external threats evoke far more fear than others more dangerous.

Consider for example violent crimes and automobiles. Violence is feared. Automobiles are lusted over. In a given year, however, there are about three times as many auto fatalities as there are murders. In a recent year the murder rate was 8.9 per 100,000. The automobile fatality rate was approximately 27.2 per 100,000. Rarely is there preoccupation with the danger inherent in a car. Random crime impacts far fewer victims, yet fear of it dramatically influences our thoughts and behavior.

We have been conditioned to fear violent crime. In one recent year there were 18,520 murders. When those perpetrated by spouses, parents killing their children, romantic triangles, lovers' quarrels, and other family killings were considered, only 5,000 remained. That means: For the average citizen there is a one-in-40,000-per-year likelihood of being involved in a fatal felony. This figure is close to the number of persons who choke to death on food or other objects each year. That figure—5,000—is less than one-third the number of people who die from a home accident.

Where do we feel safest? Where does fear abound? In the home. We come into our sanctuary, triple lock our doors, turn on our burglar and fire-alarm systems, and burn our night lights. Amid all this security, we trip, stumble, and fall to death far more often than we are assaulted.

The statistics and our fears are inproportionate. Why then do we fear that which is less dangerous, and feel more comfortable around that which is more threatening? It is because of our conditioned responses.

There is nothing dramatic enough about choking to death on a piece of steak to merit a movie being made of it. There is little dramatic about falling in the bath tub and killing yourself to deserve a book being written about it. There is not much to commend these events to the media. The sordid, surly, sadistic crimes of violence have become our entertainment appetite. The public has been fed a steady diet to nourish its neuroses.

A key study among children suggests that television is a cause of paranoia. Two thousand children, ages 7 to 11, and more than 1,700 parents were interviewed. University researchers learned that children who watch television four or more hours a day were twice as likely as other children to "get scared often." A media that deals with the sensational and sensuous will produce warped audiences. The average American spends twenty hours a week watching television! The average set is on nine hours a day. That is about one and one-half months a year spent watching television. A senior graduating from high school spent about 10,800 hours in the classroom. That same youth has watched television an average of 20,000 hours before reaching age 18. That child probably receives less than 500 hours of religious instruction.

One network executive has observed that there is one thing found to be common in most successful television presentations. That is, "the leading character's occupation is somehow connected with death."

Studies in sensory perception reveal that about 14 percent of what we learn comes through the ear, and an additional 82 percent is received through the eye. When appealed to simultaneously in an integrated way, these two senses impact 96 percent of one's attention-memory potential.

The time absorbed in and the technique used reveals how we program ourselves to fear many things. The fantasies to which we expose ourselves subconsciously groom our fears. They stroke our phobias.

We Furnish the Material

Unpredictability causes fear. This characteristic makes fear continual. If there is no indication when one is entering or exiting a fear zone, there is no time to relax. If what is feared can come suddenly and without warning, it produces a greater degree of strain. There is no period of relaxation. Though one is reasonably safe statistically from street violence, it is highly unpredictable. It can happen to anyone at anytime. The odds against it are good, but the possibility of it is ever present. We have less fear of the shower or car because the times and places of potential danger are somewhat predictable. A person can avoid, or at least get away from, the danger posed by them. There is a safety zone. When not in the shower or car, one feels safe from any danger presented by them. However, violent crime is a potential anywhere at anytime. The fear is constant. The time factor multiplies the threat. Even though the threat is less, the time factor enlarges the dread.

Some people fear flying, not because of the occasional rough air, but because when a crash will occur is unpredictable. A ride in the car on a bumpy road may be much rougher. The holes in the road can be seen in advance and thus anticipated. In flight, clear air turbulence (CAT) is always possible. The CAT makes flight unpredictable and causes fear for some. One's coping capacity is kept on alert in flight and fear often results.

Unfamiliarity also causes fear.

The lack of a clearly defined place where it won't or can't happen heightens the anxiety. A feeling that there is no place or time that we are perfectly safe makes this type of fear chronic. It can develop as an unremitting anxiety. There is no natural relief from such fear.

When one is driving a car on a bumpy road there is a feeling of being in control. There is an air of "I can make a difference." On a commercial flight there often develops a sense of "I am not in control and no matter what happens I can't make a difference." Conditions are unpredictable and uncontrollable—hence, fear.

Wherever there is the unpredictable, there is the seed of fear. Who can look at the condition of the world and not be concerned about what today's children might have to go through? Who lives without someone as the apple of his eye? Who does not have things he cherishes, things good and precious in life? Who does not have something or someone whose removal would make life's days darker? Who does not feel that change might at any moment rearrange life? It is known that momentary change can make life virtually unbearable. Any person who looks forward to what might be occasionally feels the fingers of fear.

Misconception: Knowledge causes fear. This popular misconception springs from faulty reasoning. Its conclusion is that ignorance is bliss. The fallacy of this concept is self-evident. Knowledge that the bite of a certain snake can be fatal causes fear in the life of one bitten by that snake. Would it be better for the victim to be ignorant of this fact or find a medical doctor who has more knowledge—knowledge of how to treat such a bite? Being aware of the approach of a speeding train might cause fear on behalf of one parked in his car on a railroad track. Knowing how to start that car and drive it off is a higher knowledge that dispels the fear. At best it is *a little knowledge* that causes fear. Greater knowledge overcomes it.

Fear often springs from ignorance. We must turn and face our fear. Look it in the eye, study its nature, learn of its origin. Find the breast on which this roaring lion was nursed. Expand your comprehension of this predator's nature. The world is yours if you can see through its pretense. The moment you see fear as a lie you have dealt it a mortal blow.

Fear is a carrion vulture. Though we might not view what it hovers over, the smell of defeat and death are there. This obscure bird puts to flight our voluntary actions. We are terrorized by the possibility of being the intended victim. Thus, self-imposed rigor mortis often sets in. Creativity and initiative tremble in the corridors of our consciences. Paralysis of productivity is produced.

Repel this interference with your excellence. Make proud choices of the productive influences which can enable you to be an overcomer. Don't allow this predator to perch on your shoulder. He can make of you a hero. A coward is not a hero. A hero is not a coward. The word "coward" carries in its very pronunciation the image of one frightened and hovering in a corner.

Let courage, like a new dawn radiating in the deep of space, burst forth with its beauty and energy. Let your soul walk with courage past the hypnotic gaze of this ravenous scavenger.

A lack of love causes fear.

Dr. Abraham Maslow, famed research analysist, estimates that the average American meets only about 50 percent of his need for love, interpersonal support, and intimacy. In the latter stages of his research, he became even more negative in his summary: "The truth is that the average American does not have a real friend in the world."

In Camus's novel, *The Fall,* the main character says of his life: "I have no friends; I having nothing but accomplices."

Fear dispels love and love dispels fear. When one loves there is always the risk of being hurt. To love means to commit yourself unconditionally and without guarantees. Thus, one becomes vulnerable. It is an act of faith. All of us have been disappointed by friends who were the object of our love. This hurts. In an endeavor to avoid being hurt, we withdraw. Some fear this hurt so much they are reluctant to love. In severe cases persons seek to protect their hearts from injury which might be inflicted by disappointment resulting from their love being rejected. This loveless life becomes a fear-obsessed life void of trust. Suspicion is the name of the watchdog greeting every would-be guest.

"Perfect love casteth out fear" (1 John 4:18). To love is the only way to maintain contact with the reality of who we are and what life is about. Without love, we become a mere football of destiny bouncing through life without a defined direction.

Psychiatrist Alfred Adler dissected the matter and analytically said of it: "All human failures spring from a lack of love—alcoholism, workaholics, depressions, suicides."

Every person has been hurt many times by objects of his

love. No person should feel he alone has been injured by friends. Once one begins to think in this manner, a defeatist complex develops. An inferiority disposition develops. Most of us have about the same number of defeats and disillusionments as the next person. It helps to know we are not the total cause of these letdowns. It says something good about us if we can "love our enemies and do good to those who despitefully use us" (cf. Matt. 5:44). The only alternative is to be sullenly bitter. That is not a viable option.

At the Mayo Clinic in Rochester, Minnesota, an experiment revealed the influence of love. A healthy dog was anesthetized. Its leg was broken and properly reset. Food and water awaited the animal at the moment of consciousness. Every provision was made for the dog during the period of recuperation. One basic instruction was given all who dealt with the dog—do not show it any love. After only a few days the dog shook with fear in his new world devoid of love. Later it refused to eat. Gangrene set in. It was apparent the dog was dying. He was once more put to sleep; the leg was treated. He was awakened and given love. At first the fear lingered. Response was slow, but soon love and affection were in the dog's heart and recovery began. Rapid recovery resulted thereafter. Love dispelled the fear caused by its absence.

In this same vein, Dr. Karl Menninger noted, "Love is the medicine for the sickness of the world."

One who does not know and experience God as a God of love lives in a fearful world. Such persons at best do not have the positive force of his love consciously working for them. Additionally, there is a negative environment where guilt and fear breed and brood. The idea of a ghoulish God who ambitiously and hopefully watches us to see our errors, failures, and sins, and exacts judgment without mercy, is enough to strike fear into anyone. The concept of a God of justice apart from grace is a frightening thought. Such imbalance of ideas about God puts one in a worldly environment where God withholds his love from us as the scientist did from the dog. Improper fear and trembling results. It affects one psychologically, physiologically, and mentally. To this fountainhead can be traced many streams of fear.

The same fearful world—that is, a world full of fear—can change the moment a person's attitude toward God changes. The circumstances and conditions may not change, but with the change of a concept fear can be overcome.

The kind of love that enables individuals to overcome fear and relate to others was written of by the apostle Paul as follows:

- *Love is patient and kind.*
- *Love is not jealous or boastful.*
- *Love is not arrogant or rude.*
- *Love does not insist on its own way.*
- *Love is not irritable or resentful.*
- *Love does not delight in evil.*
- *Love rejoices in the right.*
- *Love bears all things*
    believes in all things
        hopes all things
            endures all things.
- *Love never ends.*

(1 Cor. 13:4-8)

The unknown causes fear.

In ancient times cartographers and mapmakers worked with limited knowledge and limited tools. They struggled to map the world. Impressively, they accomplished much. They employed one common practice. When they came to the end of their knowledge of their small, known world, they would write on their maps: "Beyond this, there be dragons!"

That inscription seems to be written across many modern minds. Beyond what is known lurks imagined dragons imposing danger or even death. These threats were not presumed to spring forth only from known sources, but mythical ones such as dragons.

Why didn't they just mark their maps "uncharted" or "Beyond this is the unknown"? That would have been honest. Instead, they assumed the unknown to be different and threatening. Much of the unknown actually proved to be extremely beautiful and exceedingly valuable. Why then did they write, "Beyond this, there be dragons"?

Their inscription reveals an old human trait to fear the unknown. There is a tendency to assume that what has not been seen or tried is threatening, or challenging at best. It actually might be most rewarding. Even moderns still distrust and fear what is unknown.

There are many ancient maps. It appears that it never occurred to a single designer to note anything optimistic about the uncharted. Beyond lay sparkling seas, sun-kissed beaches, lush forests, majestic mountains, continents of friendly natives, rivers of gold, and other treasures of nature. All were feared because they were unknown.

Perhaps those mapmakers knew they themselves were not going beyond the known, and they did not want anybody else to do it either. They might well have been like a frightened child who, not being willing to go into a dark room, wants to divert attention from his own fear and tells other children of the threats awaiting them inside.

This basic fear factor is why many people won't venture or take risks that could greatly improve their lives. In a word, it is—fear.

In this chapter several references have been made to the effect made on the body by fear. The mind and the body are interrelated. Each affects the other. It is likely that the mind has more influence over the body than the reverse.

Montaigne, the French essayist, wrote, " . . . imagination produces the event." The mind moves the body. Some areas of the brain control even our reflexive actions such as breathing. This basic fact reveals that other more defined actions of the body also originate in the brain. Many of our actions are consciously initiated by a thought. The simple act of making a fist begins with the mind's sending a message to the muscular system to respond according to its wish. A fist results.

Dr. Paul G. Thomas, in his book *Psychofeedback,* suggests an experiment which further indicates the message-sending capacity of the mind. Try it.

Take a piece of paper and draw a circle on it about six inches in diameter. Dissect the circle with lines at right angles to each other. Number the points where the lines intersect the circle one through four, beginning at the top and moving clockwise. Obtain a piece of light string twelve to fourteen inches long. Attach a small metal object, such as a three-quarter inch plumber's washer or a key to one end. Sit at a table.

Place the paper on the table with number one away from you. Place your elbow on the table near number three. Hold the string between your thumb and forefinger directly over where the two lines cross, about one-half inch above it. Make sure the elbow is comfortable. Do not move your hand. Look at the weight. Do not take your eyes off it. Now, imagine that the weight is moving backward and forward between points one and three. Do not move your hand. Keep your eyes fixed on the weight. Fix your mind on the movement of the object back and forth. Soon the movement will begin. The amount of movement obtained will depend on your ability to concentrate.

The nerve ends will pick up the message from the brain and transfer it to the string. The mind can thus be seen to influence the nerve ends. Basically, the body can't tell the difference between the imagined and the real experiences of life. Thus, imagined fear can impact a body as much as the pain imagined.

Presently, there is in use an artificial hand that works similarly. Consider the mind to be a bio-computer. The bio-electrical hand is attached to nerve cells. The mind imagines a movement and the bio-current flows to the nerve ends which activate the mechanical hand to respond accordingly.

Likewise, the emotion of fear causes the glands of the body to be activated. When overactivated, certain glandular secretions can cause adverse physical reactions. Stress, fatigue, and actual illness can result. *Fear knots* are produced.

Having considered some of the mechanical factors creating fears, let's now consider their ultimate source.

"For God hath not given us the spirit of fear; but of power, and of love, and of a sound mind" (2 Tim. 1:7).

The gift, *charisma,* given by God is not that of a craven fear. The Greek word used is *deilia,* literally meaning "cowardice" or "fearfulness." The word "spirit" used with "fear" evidently refers to a disposition of the mind. God does not want his people to be subject to slavish fears. Many religions are based exclusively on fear. The fear which is not given by God is the fear that God is our enemy. It prompts us to act cowardly when confronted by God's enemies.

The fear not given by God gives rise to panic. A young soldier wrote of his experience on the battlefield: "How infectious fear is; how it grows when yielded to; and how, when once you begin to run, it soon seems impossible to run fast enough; whereas, if you can manage to stand your ground, the alarm lessens, and sometimes disappears." That is precisely what the Lord wants to help happen in the lives of his people.

There are two giant steps away from fear as prescribed in the Scriptures.

"What time I am afraid, I will trust in thee. In God will I praise his word, in God I have put my trust; I will not fear what flesh can do unto me" (Ps. 56:3-4).

That is a starting point. Acknowledge that there are times when you are afraid. Confess it to yourself. Then resolve in these moments to fix your mind on Christ. Realizing that, "Thou wilt keep him in perfect peace, whose mind is stayed on thee; because he trusteth in thee. Trust ye in the Lord forever; for in the Lord Jehovah is everlasting strength" (Isa. 26:3-4).

3
How Not to Fear

Centuries ago Aesop chronicled a fable revealing the seat of fear. It is the story of a mouse that dwelt near the house of a magician. The poor creature lived in constant distress because of the fear of a cat. The magician, taking pity on the mouse, turned him into a cat. Immediately the cat, formerly mouse, began to suffer from fear of a dog. The magician accommodated the cat by turning him into a dog. Then the dog began to suffer from fear of a tiger. The magician, in disgust, commanded: "Be a mouse again. As you have only the heart of a mouse, it is impossible to help you by giving you the body of a noble animal."

"Fear not" strikes at the heart of fear. Most often the expression exists in a verb tense which literally means to stop doing that which is already being done. It is an encouragement to those who are already afraid to stop. Look carefully, and you will note it is couched in reason. Fear is illogical. There are logical reasons for not fearing. These "fear nots" are intended to build courage. The word "courage" comes from the Latin root *cour*. It is a reference to the condition of the heart. Richard Coeur de Lion was the title given King Richard who allegedly had a heart like a lion. He was called "Richard the Lion-hearted." That was the condition of his heart. Fear is a heart condition that can be cured.

Courage is the result of faith, tempered by knowledge, laced with love, enlightened by moral discernment, and seasoned by experience. Where courage is domiciled, fear trembles to tread.

An Antidote for Fear

"Fear nots" are most often accompanied by "how nots." Encouragement regarding how to avoid fear is needed. Every person needs to know how not to fear. "Dragons" roam along the shadowy back roads of our minds. Nightmares are stabled in our bed chambers. Trolls hide beneath our bridges. Skeletons rattle in our closets. There are phantoms in the shaded pasts. Wolves howl in the distant hills of our tomorrows. "Please tell me how not to fear!" comes the impassioned plea.

Everyone must deal with fear. The question is "how?" Some basic steps to overcoming fear are:

- *Admit your fear.*
- *Identify your fear.*
- *Analyze your fear.*
- *Isolate your fear.*
- *Address your fear head-on.*

Now begin to apply pressure on your fear rather than letting it put pressure on you. Some helpful ways of doing this are:

- *Pray about it.*
- *Search the Scriptures regarding it.*

- *Talk to mature, understanding friends about it.*
- *Saturate your mind with Bible promises.*
- *Make direct application of Scripture to the situation.*
- *Resolve to demonstrate faith in fighting fear.*

Above the mantel of Hinds' Head Hotel in England hangs this inscription: "Fear knocked at the door. Faith answered. No one was there."

Our most threatening adversaries are not deadly germs, nuclear warfare, or savage beasts—but thought-paralyzing fears that poison the mind and erode character. *There is only one adequate shield against fear. It is faith.*

Faith disinfects the mind of doubt. It serves as a distillate for reason. Without it, fear has the key to every room in one's soul. This intemperate tenant always locks and unlocks the wrong doors at the most inappropriate times.

Jesus Christ's birth narrative assembled a cast of characters who reveal some "how not" characteristics. In each instance faith was one of the most pivotal factors.

An associated miracle involved the priest, Zacharias, and his beloved wife, Elisabeth (cf. Luke 1:1-25,36-37,40-45, 57-80). This saintly, elderly couple loved the Lord faithfully and served him loyally. A sudden hush from heaven happened four-hundred years before their miraculous experience. For four centuries there had been no message from God. No prophet had come forth to proclaim, "Thus saith the Lord . . . . " To our knowledge no living person had been visited by an angel during that period. Such experiences were buried in antiquity and recorded on faded scrolls. The passing of time had caused memories of heavenly visits to fade.

Years earlier the Lord God had revealed prophetically that he would send forth Messiah preceded by a forerunner (Isa. 40). Expectantly, society had awaited the fulfillment of that promise. Hope had waned and dimmed. Only the most faithful could envision it happening in such a bleak era.

Zacharias was serving his shift as priest in the house of the Lord. His routine duties were interrupted by an angel dramatically appearing. His awe truly was no less than ours if such an angelic being revealed himself to us. In this startled state the old priest listened to the strange message revealed to him. In stunned delight he heard the good news. Messiah was coming. Preceding this miracle another was to occur. It was announced to Zacharias that his elderly wife, Elisabeth, would also conceive and bear a child. He was to be named *John.* His life's mission was to be that of the prophesied forerunner.

Before announcing this good news the angel put Zacharias a bit more at ease with a message of assurance: "Fear not, Zacharias, for thy prayer is heard . . . " (Luke 2:13). This confirmation was needed. In the preceding verse we are told Zacharias was "troubled and fear fell upon him." It takes but little imagination to realize he must have been nearly crushed by the tonnage of fear which fell on him. In a traumatic state he heard gladly the reaffirmation, "Fear not."

Fear still tracks individuals. You sensed its hot breath on your neck. It may have come when you were at home alone. The night was quiet. There was no one near—then an uncertain sound. Your sense of hearing was alerted. Surely, there was no one there. Your own breathing deepened. You listened as the padded feet of fear stalked you. Fear had interrupted a beautiful and tranquil setting.

Students feel fear. Study has been long and hard.

Preparation has been thorough. Every effort has been made to prepare for that big test. Calm confidence is aborted by recall of how tough your professor is. His opening-day lecture introduction comes to mind, "Some of you have taken this course, thinking it is going to be an easy way to pick up a few grade points. Before you leave this class you would gladly exchange it for a case of leprosy!"

Even with all the preparation, the thought of this professor's hard testing results in a fear wave that would register on the Richter Scale.

Business persons know fear. Perhaps looming ahead there is a major project which has been worked on for a long time. A consolidated effort has been put forth to be ready for it. Then fear strikes, "Have I done everything I should have? What if I fail?" The wily wolf of fear nearly chokes you to death in such a moment.

Parents experience fear. Perhaps it has been a leisure evening. The children are at a party. Near the hour of midnight the phone rings. You are reluctant to reach for it. Fear virtually freezes your hand. Bad news is anticipated. Fear struts in your mind.

Fear of the future is activated by daily prophecies of doom. Newscasts and press releases stimulate fear. The future seems as fragile as a porcelain figurine. Doubt and despair develop. Questions emerge. Will inflation engulf us? Will recession overcome us? Will there be international conflict? Will there be a nuclear holocaust? Where is our country going? Is there a future?

Fear of the past overshadows many. Apprehension that a haunting past will eventually catch up with you activates fear. Consternation over an unflattering past causes many to fear. Will the past emerge to ruin you today?

Present-tense fear exists in many lives. Again questions are asked. Can I cope? Do I have the ability to compete? Can I relate? Do I have what it takes to get along in this society?

To a person with those and other puzzling questions, an angel of the Lord consoled, "Fear not."

It is likely that Zacharias's fear was not caused by a lack of faith. Rather, it was probably produced by what he saw. Perceptive fear, fear that is caused by the five senses, often prevails over spiritual reasoning. So, it is important to maintain one's spiritual equilibrium by keeping a biblical perspective.

There are three dramatic "fear nots" in Luke's account of Christ's birth.

You Are Being Heard (Prayer)

First was the one spoken to Zacharias. Incorporated in it is the reason why not to fear: "Thy prayer is heard." This should be a reassuring and undergirding principle in the life of every person who has faith.

By the laws of biogenetics it was impossible for the prayer of Zacharias and Elisabeth to be answered. For years they had prayed for a child. Heaven had been mute in response. Then the announcement that the prayer had been heard accorded a thrill.

Your prayer has been "heard." In the Greek this is first aorist passive indicative. That simply means your prayer is timeless. Your prayer was heard in times past when offered; it is continuing to be heard today with the result that it will be answered. This reveals the perpetual present tense of prayer.

Persons frequently pray and almost instantly complain that God did not hear their prayers. Such negative reaction is common when there is no immediate response from God.

God hears and frequently wisely delays in answering. If all answers came as immediately as thunder after lightning, we would lose our perspective. Instead of looking to the One to whom we pray, we would become even more materialistic and look for the things about which we pray. The waiting period is often a conditioning time in which God allows us opportunity to demonstrate our patience and evidence our trust. Immediacy in answering all prayer would cause us to become wrapped up in the answer to the prayer, rather than the One who answers the prayer. The delay is often used as a magnet drawing us to God. In this manner the delay is a far greater blessing than the answer.

Zacharias and Elisabeth had prayed for a child throughout their marriage. The prayer was answered in the birth of John.

A study of these three names reveals facets of God's character.

Zacharias means "Jehovah Remembers."

Elisabeth means "The Oath of God."

John means "The Favor of God."

Together they mean Jehovah remembers the oath of God, and the result is the favor of God.

His oath was to send a forerunner. Hundreds of years earlier he had made such a commitment. He remembered his oath. The result was the favor of God—John, the forerunner.

In the Bible, God has made at least 7,000 promises to every believer. God has repetitiously gone on record by committing himself to his followers. Don't you forget

Jehovah remembers the oath of God with the result being the favor of God. This favor relates to you. Revel and rejoice in this refreshing reality. Don't get tied into a *fear knot*.

You may have forgotten many of your prayers. God hasn't. What he has promised he will fulfill.

In Scotland, there lived a quiet, elderly saint in poverty. She had just spent her last few coins for food. This left her penniless and soon to be without a morsel to eat.

In her community lived several young pranksters. One day, as they passed her cottage, they heard her praying for bread. Quickwitted as they were, they devised a scheme. The next day at her appointed time of prayer they climbed up on her roof. Wrapped in a brown paper bag they had a loaf of bread. They listened as she prayed. When she made her request for bread they dropped the bread down the chimney. It landed on the hearth with a thud, disrupting her prayer.

Upon opening the package and seeing the bread she shouted with joy. Gleefully and gratefully she began to dance around the room, praising the Lord. Down from the roof came her tormenters and instantly rapped on her door. Upon opening it she found the laughing boys who explained that it was they, not the Lord, who dropped the bread down the chimney. She, with a wry smile on her face, quipped, "I asked God for bread and he gave me bread, even if he did let the devil deliver it."

Sometimes God's deliveries come disguised. We should never be blind to them and ever praise him for them.

Among all the enemies of the human race, fear is one of the worst. For this reason "fear not" echos with near monotonous repetition in every part of the Bible. It is because it is needed. A favorite, unwitting trick played by the well-balanced and well-blessed on those who are fear struck is to say, "Just pull yourself together and you will be all right." There is nothing the fearful had rather do than pull themselves together. That adds further to their frustration. They have tried with the success of one who tries to pick himself up by his boot straps. A reason and resource must be provided for overcoming fear. Effective prayer is a viable one. "Men ought always to pray and not to faint" (Luke 18:1b).

You Are a Choice Product

The second "fear not" that can untie fear knots, recorded in Christ's birth narrative, was spoken to Mary (cf. Luke 2:26-35,38-56).

As a young virgin, she unsuspectingly was engaged in one of her daily chores when this drama occurred. As was her custom, she came to the well to draw water for her family. Amid this tranquil isolation an angel of the Lord appeared to her.

As Dr. Luke recorded, the incident (Luke 1:28-30) he made note of her being "troubled at his saying, and cast in her mind . . . . " Her response as noted was to the angel's statement that she was "highly favoured," meaning she had received favor. God was giving her his free and unmerited grace in a unique measure. Her reaction revealed her to be of modest and humble mind. Feeling that she was not suited for such a fortunate message, she suffered instant mental agitation. Yet, the fact that she considered the statement calmly shows she had no hysterical excitement because of the angel's words. Her awareness of her humble role in life, coupled with a sense of personal unworthiness, caused her shock.

Lovingly, the angel stroked her spirit with a reassuring "fear not."

As always, there must be a reason for not fearing. Mary's reassurance is applicable to every person. Her role was to be distinctive. For this reason most persons can easily see how the angel's report related to her, " . . . thou has found favour with God."

This same exaltation to Mary is relevant to every person. God makes no blurred, cheap, carbon copies. You are unique in all the world. As no two snow flakes are alike, so you are distinct from all other human beings. You are rare— therefore valuable. Just as no two leaves are alike, so neither are any two persons. Diamonds are valuable because of their scarcity. You are of inestimable value because you are an original. No one can duplicate your worth. Distinctly, you stand alone as a peculiar object of God's favor.

The angelic utterance translated "favour" was *charos*. It is also the root word for our word, grace. The statement simply meant, "Mary, you are the object of God's kindness." *You* are the object of God's kindness!

Amid the most adverse circumstances be mindful you are an object of God's kindness. Things may not work out all right, but by trusting the Lord *you* will be all right. Conditions of life may have you hemmed in or penned down, but you are an object of God's favor. Friends may have disappointed you. Loved ones may have broken your heart, but you are an object of God's favor.

Even the uniquely begotten and distinctly favored Son of

God knew pain caused by friends' apathy and enemies' accusations. Yet, even in his hour of isolation on the cross, he still clung to personal faith as from the depths of despair he cried out, "My God . . . ." Though forsaken because of our sins being laid on him, he still used the personal pronoun, "*My* God."

It may appear that life's circumstances have conspired against you. All roads may be dead ends and all alleys blind. That says nothing about you, only about conditions. Amid adversity it is affirming to reflect on the fact, "You are the object of God's kindness."

Christianity is an exciting adventure. It is not a matter of ups and downs, but of ins and outs. Christ in you is the hope of glory. Faithfulness and joy amid adversity result from incarnation—not just Christ, God incarnate in the historical Jesus, but *Christ incarnate in you.* There is a delightfully different thought. Biblically, Christ is spoken of as being *in* believers. Thus, he is represented as being incarnate (cf. Gal. 2:20). This adds to your uniqueness. It evidences your favorable status. Therein is expressed his kindness to you.

A balloon's ascent is not dependent upon its color, size, or shape. What's in it counts! If helium fills it, the result is different than if mere breath fills it. Helium is lighter than air. Resultantly, it will rise into the air. A helium-filled balloon takes on the characteristic of that which fills it. You, a believer, take on the quality of Christ when he is allowed to fill you. That is, when he controls you, life takes on his characteristics. You become identified with his traits. When he is in a person, that life becomes bouyant and rises above the winds of adversity.

As with the balloon, so with you—your color, size, and shape do not matter. Your looks, wealth, degrees, or pedigree matter not. You—regardless—are the object of God's kindness. Rejoice! Fear not.

Don't be like a window shopper who appreciates but never appropriates what is beheld. God's Word was never meant for your scrutiny or mere study, but for your support. Accept the fact: You are an object of God's kindness.

Your life may seem like a 33⅓-RPM record being played at 45 RPMs. But you are an object of God's kindness. Life may be such a rat race that you are taking cheese-flavored tranquilizers. But you are an object of God's kindness.

Your hectic involvement may have you as bewildered as the person who was asked, "What do you think of civilization?" Perplexed, came the answer, "It's great, why doesn't somebody start it." That may be your neighborhood. But you are the object of God's kindness.

You may feel pursued by monsters whose heads and hands have outgrown their hearts. In this modern, madhouse you are an object of God's kindness. Fear not!

The next time you get tied in fear knots, stop and reflect on God's kindness. Forget it and remain bound. By your applying basic Bible insights, life can gain stability.

As a loving parent kindly guides a beloved child by the hand through a dark corridor, so the Lord will guide you. You are an object of his kindness, even in the dark.

You Have a Present Partner

The third "fear not" involved in the birth of Christ is recorded in Luke 2:10.

No more placid pastoral scene exists than that cradled amid the hills near Bethlehem. David had watched his sheep graze that scape. Ruth and Naomi had expressed their mutual devotion here centuries earlier. Both of these events combined could not compare with what happened there in the lives of some lowly shepherds.

Night there was so quiet it seemed to hold its breath. Night's black velvet curtain had been drawn across the sky and penned in place by the stars. Sheep seemed to freeze in their places when night enveloped the countryside. This familiar isolation was disrupted by an angel appearing to the shepherds. These desert dwellers were the most unsuspecting and unlikely prospects for an angelic visit.

God's radiant glory in the person of the angel became visible to them, as it had to Moses in the burning bush, to the Israelites in the pillar of fire in the desert, and as it would later to the three disciples on the mountain of transfiguration. Overcome by this sudden and unexpected supernatural event they were described as being "sore afraid."

Shepherds were hardy outdoorsmen. Doubtless they had fought often with wild beasts. Such fierce combat evoked little fear. Their nights had exposed them to mysterious eclipses, shooting stars, and auroras. No night had ever provided the excitement of this eventful one.

They were described as being "sore afraid," meaning they were panic-stricken. To arrest their apprehension the angel announced, "Fear not." A sigh of relief must have followed.

John records that thirty-three years later Pilate spoke of Christ, "Behold the man." To the shepherds the angel was saying, "Behold the truth the man is going to embody." That is good tidings.

The good news was that Jesus Christ was going to reveal God to us. In the pending birth God would come close enough to express his love for us, give guidance, comfort us in our sorrows, and relieve our stresses. In the person of Christ, this would be done.

Don't be afraid. God is now here to untie your fear knots. The only knots he ties are love knots.

Out of their dark and foreboding fear came jubilation. This often-repeated pattern is traceable throughout the Scriptures. Jacob lost the apple of his eye, Joseph, only to have opened to him the granaries of Egypt in a time of famine. Saul, stricken blind, had his eyes opened to new and exciting truths. A ship on which Paul was a passenger broke into pieces on the rocks of Melita to afford life preservers for 276 passengers. Their safe arrival on the beach was a stirring announcement that God delivers his distressed.

God lives. Even in our abysses of agony, he lives. A friend who spent nine years as a "guest" of the Viet Cong in the "Hanoi Hilton" told me part of his story. He said, "When you have been beaten, abused, bound, blindfolded and thrown into a dark, damp, stinking hole to serve as mosquito food, you need God. You don't need a God who is remote in the heavens. You need a God who is there with you." He concluded, "He was." That is what the angels were trying to tell the shepherds; that is what they are trying to tell us. In the person of Christ, God was and is with us.

Fear Gives Way to Action

A part of the reason for not fearing, as expressed by the angel, is there is *great joy* for you. Their joy came when their fear gave way to action. Upon hearing the message of God they applied it and acted. They went into Bethlehem. This was a dramatic action for them. Even to this day the

Bedouins who live in those same fields rarely go into town. They are looked upon as suspect by townspeople. That is why the Scripture tells us the people wondered at those things told them by the shepherds.

Right action helps overcome fear. Conversely, fear paralyzes proper action. Whether reflexive or forced action is essential to break fear's grip, if frightened, don't withdraw. Such action can give the imagination time to become hyperactive. A runaway imagination only intensifies fear. Intimidate your fear. Don't allow it to intimidate you. Take the initiative; act on it. Don't let it act on you. Do what you know you should do. By becoming involved, the shepherds confirmed their faith and assassinated their fear. The same technique works today.

The action of the shepherds was physical. Even this, however, was preceded by mental action. An act of the will was involved. Not all of our action in response to fear has to be physical. Some of it must always be mental. Act mentally on what you know. This involves summoning the will into action. It means mustering the courage and will power to act. Such involvement evidences faithful trust. Reliance like this pays spiritual dividends. It displaces a cowardly attitude with one of willful, bold idealism. Both can't be tenants in the same mind. Each is self-excluding of the other. The one will remain in residence that you will allow as an occupant.

In the wonderful world of make-believe, a tornado swept across the Kansas plains and whisked away a girl named Dorothy. In the fantasy world into which she was carried she met some interesting characters. Along the Yellow Brick Road she met a tin man who wanted a heart, a scarecrow who desired a brain, and a lion who wished for courage. They traveled together to visit the wonderful Wizard of Oz.

He helped each of them see that they already had what they most wanted within themselves. It was there all along.

By God's grace we already have within us what is needed in order not to fear. We need a heart, a brain, and courage. When fear next dances on your face, use all three. Engage your emotions, your intellect, and your will. An intellectual act of the will can change your emotions. In engaging all three, remember you can change your mind, if you will do so, in an instance. Emotions respond much more slowly. Give your emotions time to catch up with your will.

Emotion is strong. It alone can overpower either the intellect and the will; success can be achieved. The will must be fed and nourished by the intellect. The intellect must be stimulated and employed by the will. Together they can enlist your emotions in overcoming fear.

"Ye are of God, little children, and have overcome them: because greater is he that is in you, than he that is in the world" (1 John 4:4). That truth is suitable for framing. Hang it on the wall of your will. Christ is within you. You already have within you what is needed to overcome even the severest fear. That is, if you haven't lost your guts to follow the Lord.

4

The Right Kind
of Fear
(Reverence of God)

Jim and Tom were toying with the idea of doing something wrong and disapproved of by their dads. Jim demurred and Tom asked, "Are you afraid your dad will find out and hurt you?" "No," was the response, "I'm afraid he'll find out and it'll hurt *him*." This wholesome filial fear is of the type appropriately due our God. It is called filial fear because it is the sentiment of an affectionate child toward a loving parent. This fear has as its source love and gratitude.

The "fear of the Lord" is an often-repeated Bible theme. In concert, Psalm 111:10 and Proverbs 9:10 remind us, "The fear of the Lord is the beginning of wisdom." Blessed intimacy with the Lord is always accompanied with reverential awe. Flippant, pretentious familiarity with him is born of ignorance of his nature.

The presence of a reverent fear of him results in the absence of all other fear. A fearless life is the product.

The British Lord Shaftesbury was spoken of as one with the right fear balance. "He feared man so little, because he feared God so much."

Any normal person with intelligence enough to understand crisis situations becomes "excited" and/or "nervous." Initially this is neither good nor bad. The use of it determines which it becomes. This excitement is neither courage nor cowardice, fear nor fright, nor anything else other than an acceleration of bodily functions intended to reinforce physical responses. It is additional strength to be used any way you choose. If used properly, they are positive sources of defense and decisive affirmation.

Fear in the Bible can be beneficial or baneful. It is friend or foe. Which is dependent upon the use of it? Arousal, excitement, and basic nervousness serve as an alarm system to arouse and alert us. Reactions vary. Some persons want to fight, some freeze, others flee, while many fear.

Fear of God is intended to be beneficial. Properly understood it is a friend.

To the ancient Hebrews, he was awesome. In reality, the Lord is. The appeal to fear him is a two-edged sword. One is restraint, the other reward. Fear of the Lord is plainly for our good. "The Lord commanded us to do all these statutes, to fear the Lord our God, for our good always, that he might preserve us alive" (Deut. 6:24). Some of the benefits derived from the fear of the Lord follow.

The fear of the Lord prolongeth days (Prov. 10:27).
The fear of the Lord is a fountain of life (Prov. 14:27).
The fear of the Lord is the beginning of wisdom (Prov. 9:10).
The fear of the Lord is instruction in wisdom (Prov. 15:33).
He will fulfil the desires of them that fear him (Ps. 145:19).
Oh how great is thy goodness, which thou hast laid up for them who fear thee (Ps. 31:19).

Those are a few of the rewards inherent in the fear of the Lord, reverence for the Lord. There are also restraints involved for our good.

> *Surely his salvation is at hand for those who fear him (Ps. 85:9).*
> *By the fear of the Lord a man avoids evil (Prov. 16:6).*
> *. . . what doth the Lord require of you, but to fear the Lord our God, to walk in all his ways, to love him, to serve the Lord . . . (Deut. 10:12).*

The Old Testament "fear of God" is understood better in light of the "love of God" in the New Testament. To fear God means to appreciate his great love for us so fully that we in turn love him so much we desire responsively and responsibly to obey him. Failure to realize this results in a foreboding fear of him.

An unknown poet gives a grim picture of a traveler, on a lonesome road, who has caught a glimpse of a frightful shape close behind him:

> *And having once turned round walks on,*
> *And turns no more his head.*

This dreaded "thing" is there. It is right on his heels. Though he does not see it, he feels it breathing down his neck. Resolutely, he rigidly fixes his gaze ahead and remains inflexible. In his heart a sickening horror is brewing. This is a depressing picture. It is, however, how many deal with their thoughts of God. They know the thought of him lingers in memory. There is an awareness of his presence. It is so graphic at times it seems a hand is soon to reach out and touch them. They rush on, refusing to turn and see the Face of love beaming on them. He is there to bless them and strengthen them. Yet, because they refuse to face him, get to know him, and lovingly respond to him, he is the terror and freezing dread of their life.

God Is Awesome, Not Awful

Fear, in the form of reverential awe, is the beginning of knowledge. The more the knowledge increases, the keener is the awareness of God's love. Gratitude for his shielding love grows.

The fear of the Lord is a much-neglected topic. Even when discussed, it is often treated with dread suspicion. When the Bible speaks of it, the reference is to a controlling motive in matters spiritual and moral. It is not a mere fear of his power or righteous retribution. It is rather a wholesome wariness of displeasing him. As such, it is a marvelous, motivational influence. It banishes the terror that would prompt us to shrink from his presence and beckons us to come closer to him.

A child definitely loved by his/her mom/dad may have this fear. In the young life it serves as a restraint preventing improper behavior. It is also a stimulus encouraging correct conduct. In this instance the parent/child love is so strong that the child wants to do what is right, lest the parent be disappointed, offended, or injured. The child fears bringing reproach on the parent. There is a fear of letting the parent down. Such fear is not of retribution, punishment, or discipline. It inspires a constant carefulness. It motivates the child to be and do his best because of the commendable expectation of the parent.

Another side of this coin is also worth investigation. It is a beautiful, positive influence. It causes a child to desire and drive to meet the high ideal of the loving parent. Assume that the parent knows more and loves stronger than the child. Such a parent would want only the best for the child. Thus, the child who fears disappointing the parent aspires to do that which is desired by the parent. This fear serves as a driving force for good.

When we fear God we desire to please him. We do so not because we tremble before his power, but because we yield to his love. Love and fear mingle with love-tempering fear. The result is reverence. This is a rare and constructive application of fear in life.

The fear of the Lord is not of his punitive power, but a fear of causing him a broken heart. In this form it serves as a defense against improper conduct.

> *Serve the Lord with fear, and rejoice with trembling (Ps. 2:11).*
> *Let all the earth fear the Lord: let all the inhabitants of the world stand in awe of him. . . . Behold, the eye of the Lord is upon them that fear him, upon them that hope in mercy (Ps. 33:8,18).*

Reverence, Not Revulsion

The Old Testament meaning associated with the word translated "fear" is revealing. There is a Hebrew word for fear which means to travail, to fear and tremble with pain and anguish of mind. This is not the one utilized of the Lord. A different word is used which means to be timorous, to venerate, to reverence, actually to worship.

He is deserving of this type fear because of his justice and holiness which none can satisfy. We should desire to exercise the right fear toward him because he lovingly mingles these qualities with his mercy and grace. This does not cause dismay but delight.

Pardon a rather mundane illustration. Have you ever watched a dog as its master returned after a slightly-longer-than-usual absence. The dog rushes mutely to its master and communicates deep affection. How? Every muscle in the dog's body becomes involved. Highly involved are the muscles near the end of the body. The tail wags excitedly. The body moves with sheer delight. The dog's eyes flash with adoration. In a moment the animal unmistakably expresses his love for his master. A loving master then showers affection on his dog.

In light of that description, the following definition of worship can be understood. It means "to do the dog to." We, the subjects, when engaged in true worship lovingly respond to and relate to our God. We are to come before our God with "fear and trembling."

We should move through the world as though it were the temple of God, and we are allowed to relate happily to him therein. Such an identity with the Creator enables us, his creation, to appreciate all of his creation.

Reverential fear in such a form is refreshing. It is an admirably positive force. One is drawn to God by such an attitude. Felt within oneself is a bit of dignity and pride because of being involved with God in a love act. Such an act lasts an eternity.

Wholesome fear of the Lord results in attraction to him—love, trust, worship, faith, fascination, adoration, reverence, respect, and piety.

One wholesome type of godly fear is seen in a patient/doctor relationship. Illustrative of this is an accident victim who has been brought into the emergency room of a hospital. The victim's condition is unknown even to himself. The doctor, a long-time friend, enters wearing a cautious smile. The examination begins.

Certain movements are painful. There are evident open wounds, some lacerations, and a broken bone. The patient/doctor friendship is of long standing, but it still hurts for the medical expertise to be applied in certain cases. The patient is apparently suffering severe pain. The doctor is aware that the suturing and bone setting will cause pain. Even the administering of some local anesthetic is painful.

All the while the doctor is doing what must be done. Perhaps he has to fight back tears occasionally. He does so to keep his eyes clear in order to perform the delicate task at hand. While working he speaks in low, comforting, reassuring tones. Sweat beads form on the brow of the patient. His doctor friend is doing what must be done to help him. Still there is fear in the heart of the sufferer. Pain is there. Medical treatment is being gingerly applied. Even though the victim knows the doctor is a knowledgeable friend who is doing what is best for his patient, there is fear of the doctor. There is also fear of what might have to be done at the hand of the doctor under the circumstances. Though there is love and knowledge involved, the pain is no less real. Pain causes fear.

In this instance there is fear associated with the doctor because of what he must do. At times we work ourselves into distinct circumstances where God being God, even though he is a loving and knowledgeable friend, must for our good relate to us in such a way as to cause pain. This pain may take any one of several forms. It is, nevertheless, pain.

We should fear putting ourselves in such a position as to force God into the role of the operating doctor. However, remember the doctor is never nearer the patient than when performing surgery.

After the emergency room treatment is completed, there is relief. Once recovery begins it rapidly covers the memory of the pain. Resultantly, there is even more respect by the patient for the doctor. There is a closer friendship. Yet, fear forged it.

In metallurgy, intense heat is required to bond two pieces of metal. Once it is forged together, it is stronger at that point than at any other. This is true of our relationship with the Lord. Sometimes there are fear-heated crises that bind us closer to God than we have ever been. Such fear is a blessing.

Love Out of the Root of Fear

Ideally, there must develop a balance between one's knowledge of and love for God and one's fear of him. A mature love for God will result in a wholesome fear of him. Fear is kept in balance by a knowledge of his full nature. Basic in his nature is the fact he always offers grace before judgment, mercy before justice. His love tempers all of his dealings with us. Were it not for these traits we might well live in terror and dread. Where such states of mind do exist, one of two things has happened. That person has either developed an imbalance in his understanding of God, or he has a legitimate guilt conscience. In the case of the latter, such fear can be a blessing if it motivates the person to respond as the Lord desires. He does not want us to see ourselves as the sinners we are and go away remorseful over guilt. He wants us to see ourselves correctly, then repent, and go away rejoicing over grace. If fear produces such a result, it is a blessing. The refreshing reward is that it turns into gratitude. Gratitude springs forth into gladness encased in joy.

To know him is to love him!

This kind of fear is not cowering fear. It is not debasing.

It elevates the mind and gives wings to one's spirit. It sets the captive free. It deflates all lower fears and gives courage to confront the challenges of life. It is not imposing, impoverishing, or imprisoning.

Have you ever felt the release resulting from a fear being dispelled? Perhaps it followed a tense moment of apprehension. Conditions may have caused the unknown to intimidate you. Then suddenly there was a revelation which exposed the assumed terror to be no threat at all. Maybe it was a dark night and you were alone. Footsteps were heard on the patio. They were thought to be some life-threatening wild beast or a blood-thirsty intruder.

At last, when you worked up the nerve to turn on the outside lights, it was only the neighbor's playful pup that had wandered over. The relief may have resulted in an immediate outburst of tears or laughter. Possibly both at once. Even now recalling it you might feel the physical release associated with the emotional relaxation coming from the dispelling of fear.

It is a good sensation. Upon reflection you might remember the intensity with which you faced the incident. That is a capsule insight into what the body of one experiences who lives in abnormal fear. One who lives with inordinate fear of God is even adversely affecting his own body, not to speak of his emotions and spirit.

When one gains a correct attitude toward God and lovingly responds to his love initiative—physical healing, emotional stability, mental peace, and neurological calm are all aided. Those are the additives to a right relationship with the Lord.

To know him and to love him is to "rejoice with trembling." It activates one to "serve the Lord with fear."

Proper fear of God is a proud prelude to peace of mind and joy. It is the discord that makes enjoyable the concord. Holy fear commends God. Such fear is not only commendable, it is commanded. It produces ardent awe. It dispels anxiety.

Never to have been in the company of a highly admired, prestigious person is to miss this understanding of awe. Fear of God legitimately causes open-mouthed awe. One marvels over the wonder of an eminent personality. It is a certain form of fear. Most persons have experienced the excitement of meeting a celebrity about which much is known. If this is an admired and respected person, a gasp of awe might be emitted—or a blush or a guffaw. There is a sense of being in the presence of excellence. This awe form of fear is far from awful.

I have been in the private company of a friend who served as president of the United States. Though he was a long-time friend, there was nevertheless a sense of awe associated with being with him. His role entitled him to my respect and esteem. Our relationship was good but our roles different. My role differed from his. Respect was at work.

When we grasp even a bit of God's role, then in awe we

gladly bow before him in wonder. This wonder is fear-clad in admiration, bowing before eminence. The Lord is, after all, God of the universe. He, the Creator, is worthy of adoration by his creatures.

The prophet Isaiah had a vision of the glory and grandeur of the Lord. He exclaimed, "Woe is me! for I am undone."

He was awestruck. Two considerations occurred to him in that moment. The first related to himself, the other to God. The concept of God always has an influence on one's self. Basic to our nature is a sense of relation to God. When we think of him we always think of self. Oneself is a part of one's thought of him. An awareness of his nature reveals his superiority. A sense of contrast came to Isaiah's mind.

God was high and lifted up. He was God. This awareness struck awe in the lowly, humble heart of the prophet. The eminence of Jehovah and the inferiority of the prophet were counterpoints not to be ignored. God's worthiness and Isaiah's unworthiness were apparent.

This kind of fear is not out of character for God's children, even in a day when such is thought by many to be out of date. A loss of this holy, reverential respect—which is a form of fear—leaves one irreverent and egocentric. Without it one is weaker. Life for such a person is void of legitimate wonder.

Egomania involves one in a small world called "self." Such a world gives little occasion for being aghast. Once Isaiah gained a proper perspective of the Lord, he enjoyed the elevation of a lofty ideal. Much depression is apparent in persons who have no updraft caused by the uplifting awe of God.

We are often transfixed by persons who have done so much more, been so many more places than we, achieved greatness, and accomplished significant goals. To be around them challenges our spirits. Extend this principle to its ultimate and there stands God. "Worthy." This worth stimulates reverential fear. There we should bow in admiration and adoration. Truly we cry "woe is me!" before him.

Such fear refreshes and challenges. It solicits respect and appreciation. The grandeur of God is fearful, awe-inspiring, and stupendous.

A Desire to Please

Fear of God in the Bible sense is godly, lovely, and refreshing. It is a matchless motivator.

A pastor chatted with a young couple he had united in marriage only a few weeks earlier. He asked the groom if the bride had burned their first meal. They laughed and she replied, "I was so afraid I would. I had heard and read so much about brides not being able to cook that I resolved to be an exception. My husband was going to have the very best meal a bride could possibly prepare for her husband. I got everything out and started early. At last, I got everything on to cook. I was afraid things wouldn't taste right. It was ready on time but he was late. I was afraid it was going to cool and ruin."

The pastor tactfully interrupted and noted she had said "afraid" three times. "Why were you afraid? Did you marry a brute?"

Cutely, flippantly she answered, "Why, of course not!" Then with adoring eyes that revealed her heart, she looked at him.

"Why then were you afraid?" kidded the pastor.

"Don't be silly. You know what I mean!"

It is apparent what she meant. Her fear was not fright. Her loving desire was to please the one to whom she had completely given herself. In this case the fear of her husband was the beginning of good cooking.

There is a difference in the fear of the Lord and being frightened of the Lord. Those who truly fear him want to serve him. There is no fright associated with this form of fear.

Knowledge Dispels Fear

Abnormal and inordinate fear of God results from not knowing him and his role.

A financially impoverished widow awaited eviction. She was far behind in her rent. Other bills had accumulated. Her utilities had been turned off and her eviction notice received.

There was a knock on her door. She cowered inside in absolute silence. Her doors were locked and her drapes drawn. In terror she heard again the knock on the door. Breathlessly, she trembled at the sound. Finally, the knocking ceased. She gained a sense of relief. Her conditions prompted her to assume it was the officials who had come to repossess her properties and put her out on the street. The knock at the door had caused her to freeze in fright.

Had she the courage to answer, she would have found to her delight quite a different situation. The knock was by her pastor. Through the grace of friends he had accumulated enough money to pay her utilities, rent, and other bills. He had come to share the good news and offer her the relief she needed. Her lack of understanding him and his role had prompted her to let fear rule.

Many people fail to understand the compassionate role of

God. Jesus Christ came into the world to pay our debts and meet our needs. He wants to be one's best friend and supporter. Compassionately, he wants to be the living fulfillment of the truth: "My God shall supply all your need according to his riches in glory by Christ Jesus" (Phil. 4:19).

Once this is understood, one can open one's heart to God and experience even greater glee than the widow would have if she had opened the door to her pastor. By keeping Christ out, one lets percolate the possibility of God's fulfilling some dread role in his life. Ignorance enables fear to grow sharp talons and long fangs. Knowledge, love, and receptivity of Christ cage this raging beast. Maturity in the Lord tames and trains it to perform productively.

We are a society of modern tent dwellers. Everyone either lives in content or discontent. Reverential fear enables one to live in content. Dread fear caused by disobedience makes one cower in discontent. One chooses one's residence.

Dean Inge, a loquacious liberal of a previous generation, observed, "There never was a time when the fear of God played so small a part as it does now. We are not afraid of God's judgment as were earlier generations. The decay of fear as an element in vital religion is one of the most significant features of our time. The disappearance of threats from the pulpit is a very remarkable phenomenon, however we may account for it. The modern churchgoer is not much afraid when he listens to the warnings of God's judgment."

If I see an impending danger, and don't warn a person whose life is endangered because I don't want to frighten that person, I would be foolish. If a warning would spare the life, the moment of fear would be justified. To remain mute in face of disaster can, in certain cases, be punishable by law. Failing to speak of the wrath of God and not warning of it is to fail our friends. The danger, though unpleasant, is real. To tell of it is not to threaten but to aid. To look the other way and not face the fact of God's wrath is folly. His wrath is tempered with mercy, grace, and love, but it cannot be denied. It should not be ignored.

One who refuses God's love and spurns his grace does well to fear the consequences. The basic good that exists in the passion of fear is to warn of danger and prompt escape from calamity. It often leads to a place of safety. Then it vanishes and leaves us there to be guided by the white-robed angel of grace. We are thereafter in company with a far better friend—mercy.

The wrath of God is only enacted after all of his exhaustive efforts of reconciliation are exhausted. He is not an intemperate or impatient demigod desirous of crushing little people. However, since he is a God of justice, he has to punish those who deserve it as a result of refusing his overtures of love. For him to be the holy God, he must be just or merciful. We choose for him.

Augustine spoke of fear as the needle, sharp and painful, but bringing in the thread; the needle passes, and the pain is gone, and then comes the thread which forms the union and joins the soul to God. Thus, fear may begin blessing to the soul, love perfects it, and then—fear all gone—grace prevails.

An innocent man has no cause to fear a judge whom he knows to be honest, knowledgeable, and fair. The integrity and intelligence of the judge give courage and reassurance to the person having no need to fear the judge's discretion. When we understand the nature of God we fear only violating his law.

"It is a grand and magnificent thing," wrote Origen, an

early church father, "always to have before the eyes of the heart the fear of God." Such fear is not only the "beginning of wisdom"—it is also the final word. There is a fear which "hath torment," but this God desires to replace with a fear born of joy. It is good for inordinate fear to be cast out and replaced by the loving favor of God.

A powerful person who defends a position can become the object of fear by those who oppose that stance. God was menacing and a terror to the enemies of Israel. His acts were considered by them "terrible acts." These acts were fearful for the enemies of Israel. For Israel they were his saving intervention. Since the Lord's mighty acts were considered terrible by those opposing his will, he himself was considered terrible. Thus, he was feared.

There comes a point in considering the "fear of God." One must admit he stands for and against certain things. Those who oppose him are in big trouble, and they ought to be full of fear. It is hoped they will be so full of fear they will change their minds, repent, and relate to him in love. Then his defense becomes theirs. That for which he stands is theirs. That which he opposes, they oppose. Once this change of attitude and commitment is made, that which was feared is seen to be proper. Every point has a counterpoint. For him to love, he must abhor the opposite. Those who identify with that which he hates are standing on the ground where his lightning is known to strike. They do well to fear— with dread terror. This terror ideally should not be an end in itself, but a motivating influence prompting one to flee to his shelter, supported by the four columns of love, mercy, grace, and forgiveness.

5
Worry—
Fantasized Fear

Epictetus, a Greek Stoic who lived during the first century AD, wisely observed a trait still prevalent today. "When you have had enough to eat today, you sit down and weep about tomorrow's food. Slave!"

That undiminished habit of worrying about tomorrow, regardless of how good today might have been, lives on. By worrying about what might be potential on tomorrow, we fail to enjoy the bliss and blessing of today. Don't diminish the delight of today by dashing it with doubt about tomorrow.

Worry is fantasized fear.

Worry is interest paid by those who borrow trouble! Worry relates to future events. It is the projection of a negative thought. Even if it relates to a past event, it is the projection of a thought about how it will affect the future. It is imagined dread related to future events. To worry is to imagine the worst and expect it to be reality. It is a cruel tyrant who enslaves millions. Many are robbed of the joy of life by fantasized fear.

It is reported that worry kills more people than work. If that is true, it is because more people worry than work. A day of worry is more exhausting than a day of work. There is a way of escaping from the worries and corroding cares of daily life. The formula is simple. It involves "Casting *all* your care upon him, for he careth for you" (1 Pet. 5:7). Give him your work, plans, life, rights, influences, responsibilities, and obligations. When you have turned everything over to him, there is nothing left for you to be troubled about!

You can't change the past by worrying about it, but you surely can ruin a perfectly good present by worrying about the future.

Worry is a world ailment that has reached epidemic proportions. Unfortunately, it is highly contagious. It is easily caught and readily spread. This ailment affects one's mind. It weakens one's ability to think clearly. It reduces the power of one's will. In some cases persons are unable to make even the simplest of decisions because of it. A paralysis of volition develops.

Fret Not

A theme which runs parallel with "fear not" is "fret not" (Ps. 37:1). We have a clear and emphatic directive not to worry. If worry achieved anything constructive, it would be worthwhile. It is not only neutral, it is negative. It occupies the computer of the brain keeping it from programming thought. The brain can think on only one primary thought at a time. If that time is occupied with worry, there is no positive flow of thought. Thus, the computer might as well be shut down. It isn't producing.

Sir Thomas More, in his work *On Fear,* wrote,

> *If evil comes not, then fears are vain;*
> *And if they do, fear but augments the pain.*

This sage wisdom affirms that worry is interest paid in advance on capital that may never be received. If you worry and the cause never materializes, you have wasted interest. If it does develop, you will have only kept yourself from proper preparation because of negative thoughts.

Worry is the projection of a negative thought into the future. Consider your mind to be a movie projector. Turn it on and it projects an image. The screen is the future. Now practice this procedure. Turn off the projector. Cease that negative thought. However, before leaving the subject, remove the negative reel. Rethread it with a positive thought on the same subject. Never let your mind leave a topic without superimposing a positive idea over a negative concept. At first this may have to be consciously done. Through consistent practice, it can become instinctive.

The positive thought always has its root in Bible truth. For this reason, Bible memorization is commended. By having on file in the memory an applicable truth, it can be drawn out and applied to a given situation in a moment's notice. Right now go ahead and hang up on the bulletin board of your mind those two simple words, "fret not." Accept them as your primary thought-patrol officer.

Two Things Not to Worry About

There are two things you should never worry about. Only two!

You should never worry about things which need changing but which you *can't change!*

- *Worry won't change that fact.*
- *Worry only erodes your vitality.*

- *Worry keeps you from some other productive endeavor.*

The other thing you should never worry about is equally as important. Never worry about things which need changing and you *can change* them!

- *If they need changing and you can do it, change them.*
- *Worry retards initiative.*
- *Worry causes abnormal and occasionally defeating reserve.*
- *Worry only delays a worthwhile project.*

If you can only be successful in ridding your life of those two areas of worry, progress will have been made. Remember: One, never worry about things you can't change. Two, never worry about things you can change. By eliminating those two roadblocks to constructive thought an avenue of productivity is opened.

Analyze the things you worry about most often. Do they fall into either category? If so, stop worrying. Either forget about those things, or get up and do what you can and should do to change them.

Don't Have a Divided Mind

Jesus saw the poor and needy shuffling about in their search for substance and he urged them not to worry.

He saw the rich groping for security and he appealed to them not to worry. The rich were suffering what Tennyson called "the narrowing lust for gold."

Four times in a brief passage (Matt. 6:25-34) Christ

appealed, "Take no thought . . . " (v. 31). He is by no means discouraging ordinary, prudent foresight. His is no appeal for a blind, irrational leap. At no time does Jesus ever hint at a shiftless, thriftless, reckless, or thoughtless attitude. He is not negating practical, prudent planning. He simply is forbidding fearful worry.

Foresight is commended. Foreboding is forbidden.

In this ancient passage, Jesus revealed that worry is putting tomorrow's possible clouds over today's sunshine. He advised, "Take no thought for the morrow" (v. 34). His was an appeal to avoid trying to handle tomorrow's possibilities while dealing with today's realities. Don't get ahead of yourself.

The Greek word translated thought is *merimnao*. It consists of *merizo* meaning "to divide" with the suffix *nous*, meaning "mind." Worry is a divided mind. "Take no thought" is an old British axiom meaning "solicitous anxiety." Jesus appeals for us not to dream up problems. Concentrate on reality and plan accordingly. Simply stated, Jesus counseled, "Don't worry!"

Worry is like a rocking chair. It gives you something to do, but it doesn't get you anywhere. It is as endless as it is useless.

Worry is like a fog; it hides more than it provides. An area seven city blocks square covered by a fog 100 feet high contains only enough water to fill an ordinary drinking glass. It obscures vision, but makes no provision for growth.

The English word "thought" used to translate the original Greek word had a different meaning than it does today. It meant anxiety, restlessness, or the penetration of fear which upsets the balance of life. It turns the whole soul into moods of dejection and weary anxiety. In light of that definition, it is easily understandable why Jesus urged persons not to approach life with such an attitude.

Historians used the same word in describing a death: "Queen Catherine died of thought." Actually, she "worried herself to death."

Cleopatra is represented as commenting to a friend, "What shall we do, Enobarbus?" His response, "Think and die." He knew worry would only lead to death. If this is not the death of a person, it is of an ideal.

Worry destroys life. Little ants pick a carcass cleaner than mighty lions. Little worries do the same.

In Jesus' statement he used birds and lilies as examples of the care of our Heavenly Father. He is careful to point out that these are far less important than you, and your Heavenly Father intimately cares for them. Instinctively, they know it.

"Fear ye not therefore, ye are of more value than many sparrows" (Matt. 10:31). If he attends the funeral of every sparrow, surely he will attend your need.

Be like an industrious bird. Get up early and get active. Energetically, do your best to be self-supporting. "His eye is on the sparrow," and you can be sure he is watching over you. He is much more than a bird watcher. He provides for the little bird. He will do the same for you. Observe the little bird carefully, however. He scratches. Compassionate care of the Heavenly Father does not lull the bird into lethargy.

Take a look at the lilies. They grow only in their place. There they grow well. They live in harmony with nature. They do not try to contradict all laws of logic and reason. They bloom where they are. You can and should do the same.

Christianity is not merely a religious experience. Neither is it a perpetual emotional high. It should not be considered a free ride through life. It is rather an interpretation of unspecifically religious events. That proper interpretation leaves no room for worry. It is an outlook on life, as well as a life-style. It is a look at life through the lenses of trust and faith. It surely looks better like that. It will give you that "lily feeling"—secure.

When you realize God cares for you, then you know you don't have to carry the cares of the world on your shoulders. God knows your load limit and will limit your load. Never fear.

It Is Illogical to Worry

A study conducted by behavioral psychologists involved an analysis of worriers. It concluded:

Forty percent of what one worries about never happens.
Thirty percent is past and all the worry in the world can't change it.
Twelve percent is needless worry about our health.
Ten percent involves petty miscellaneous matters.
Eight percent deserves our consideration.

If you can't be 100 percent worry-free, it would make you far more productive if you could be only 92 percent. That would allow you to give your best efforts to the 8 percent deserving your attention. This would prevent dissipation of energy and frustration of effort. A key factor in success is properly to divide the right 92 percent from the proper 8 percent. The person who does it best succeeds most often.

One of the few lines of logic favoring worry goes as

follows. "Don't tell me that worry, fear, and anxiety don't work! I know better! The things I worry about, fear, and get anxious over, just never happen! So it is effective and productive."

Mark Twain, in his waning years, noted, "I am an old man and have known many troubles, but most of them never happened."

We can build for ourselves cages of misery by always looking on the dark side. Worry is the sentinel standing guard at the door of such a cage. With the same mind we fear and fret, we can think reasonably and enjoy the resultant composure. The same mind that produces peptic ulcers can become a seedbed for "peace that passes understanding" (cf. Phil. 4:6-7). This cruel tyrant, worry, can be dismissed and discharged by a mere change of thought patterns.

More Antidotes

Try these antidotes for worry!

Never worry over hearsay or rumors. It does no good to worry about something that might not even be true. First, get the facts.

Years ago when the lovely community of Marietta, Georgia, was being settled, a hostile relationship built up between the settlers and the local Indians. The settlers decided on a signal in the event there was possible danger. Uncle Jimmy Anderson was appointed to blow a certain signal on his fox horn if peril were pending.

Late one evening the community was alarmed to hear the warning. As preplanned, they rushed to the town square and gathered in a fortified warehouse. Fearfully, they awaited an attack by the Indians. Shortly after midnight, a store next to the fortress caught fire. They just knew the Indians were responsible and anticipated the worst. Anxiety developed for fear that a torch would be set to their fortification. The long hours of the night dragged feverishly into the light of dawn. The approach of day only increased certainty that with the coming of light there would be an all-out attack.

Dawn came with all of its quiet, radiant beauty. There was no attack. Cautiously, a scouting party was sent out with fond farewells to find the entrenched enemy. They found the nearest Indians about twenty miles away. They were happily encamped on the opposite bank of the Chattahoochee River. The Indians were blissfully enjoying productive activities with no thoughts of going on the warpath. The entire fiasco was a false alarm. The terror was intensified by what must have been an accidental fire caused by a rodent.

All night long they had lived in dread terror, simply because they did not have the facts. Truth would have dispelled worry.

Define your worry problem. Generalities need to be exchanged for specifics. It is much easier to hit a bull's-eye on a target with a rifle than with a scatter gun. Get on target. Know the issue. Don't allow your mind to get so involved with fantasy that you fail to see the fact you must deal with. Thoughtfully analyze the problem. Quacks treat symptoms. Doctors treat diseases. Once a disease is cured, the symptoms go away. Cosmetic covering of symptoms only allows a disease time to spread. Deal with the disease. Is it a person, a thing, an act, or an attitude?

Think about only one thing at a time. Negative thoughts

have a tendency to swarm like bluefish around one of their own caught on a hook. One at a time you can handle problems. Collectively, they can become ponderous. Isolate your problems and deal with them one at a time. You might want to climb several trees in a forest, but never try to climb but one at a time! Never climb a tree until you get to it.

In the developing years of our country, a traveler was worried about crossing a river he realized was ahead. He met a settler and asked him if he knew of the river and could give him any pointers about crossing it. "Yep, I do," was the reply, "and there's one thing I've learned about. Never cross it till you get to it."

Take your problems as they come. Deal with them one at a time. Some couplets have lived for years because of their simple truth.

> *Life by the yard is hard.*
> *Life by the inch is a cinch.*

Phase your plans. Plan your phases.

Make a Worry Diary

Worry makes life more difficult for you and those around you. If you tend to fear the future, remember it is seldom as bad as you think. If some evil does come hurtling down upon you, there is being prepared for you—right now—the strength you will need to confront it when it arrives. It is futile to worry about these fantasized fears because if they do arrive you shall have depleted your strength before they show up. Thus, you will be left drained and unable to contest them.

If we had the capacity to replay previous thoughts and

prior events, the sequence might amaze us. Try to reconstruct your worst problem of last week. Recall how you thought of it the week prior as it approached. Was it as bad as you envisioned? Likely not.

Why not make a case study right now? What is your biggest current worry? Write it down. Give some detail to what your worst fear is regarding it. Spell out what you are most worried about. Give identity to it, such as: When will it happen? What will happen? How painful and difficult will it be? Who will suffer most? What will be the lasting impact on you? Keep this log. When this dreaded event is history again, review it. In retrospect, ask the same questions. After it has occurred, compare the anticipation with the realization.

People have long realized that good things, when imagined, are seldom as good when realized. This principle has been canned in this cliche: "Anticipation is always better than realization." Conversely, regarding worry, "Worry is always worse than reality."

Worry Bars from the Best

Most of the bars that serve as barriers to you have been self-imposed. You put them there! If you put them there, you can remove them. Your greatest restraints are mentally self-superimposed. Fear in the form of worry imposes rigid restraints. Persons demur and refuse to venture because of worry. It forms a barrier just as formidable as bars on a jail cell.

Certain birds mark off territories that belong to them. The cardinal is one that does. There is no visible territorial boundary to the human mind. The bird knows its territory and stays within it. Ornithologists have observed a cardinal fly up to its territorial boundary and stop as suddenly as if it had flown into a glass window. It knows its limit. Though the bird has the capacity to fly further, it will not go beyond the boundary because of a self-imposed cage.

Worry builds such restraints for humans. They are fearful to go beyond a certain point. Capacity is not the restraint. Worry is. Persons worry about untried ability, untreaded territory, unknown truths, and unseen adversaries. Imagining them to be worse than they are, they are uncontested. In this manner, worry is an easy winner.

It is better to have your rights and opportunities taken away from you by a foreign dictatorial power than to forfeit them because of fantasized fear—worry.

Worry constructs mental bars. Ask any physician to describe the result of worry. He will tell you plainly that it weakens the body, lowers the energy level, lessens resistance, interrupts normal bodily functions, and—if unchecked and unchallenged—it will result in physical illness.

Worry builds bars limiting the function of the mind. In addition to preventing you from doing your best, it limits calm and quiet. It is an agitant to a peaceful heart. Worry undermines courage, creates suspicion, breeds doubt, feeds mistrust, leads to seeking sinister motives behind innocent actions, and allows for a gloom-and-doom attitude. It brews a bitter cup of pessimistic tea.

One of the best things about bars being self-imposed is: If you put them up, you can take them down. You, having allowed yourself to develop this worry complex, can reverse it. It is an inside job. Just as you have developed a worry pattern by habitually thinking a certain way, so you can reverse the process of changing your mind.

Do you want to change? Change your wants! "Repent" is a word found throughout the Bible. Simply defined, it means to change your mind. A reversal of attitude is involved. This is needful regarding any and all sin. It is applicable regarding worry.

Thought patterns begin with a thought; that's elementary, dear Watson, isn't it? Sequential thoughts of a kindred nature are added until a trend develops. At first, this may be induced by outside influences such as a friend, a book, an experience, or a simple idea. At a moment like this a thought pattern can be changed. If you are a worrier, etch on the metal of your mind this simple fact, "fret not." That is a thought—one thought. Now by adding related Bible and other positive attitudes, you can start a string of anti-worry thoughts. By doing so, bars begin to bend. With continued, internal, positive pressure they can be broken. The invisible worry wall can come down. You can release your new optimism, faith, and trust. An adventurous new you can walk through the hole in the wall into a productive and positive future.

It is not only important to decide upon doing it, but to set a time for doing it. We cannot live without weaknesses, fears, and worries. If that be true, we must fight it out with them. If so, why not here and why not *now*! Start now.

Worry Chokes

In a big, unabridged dictionary somewhere down the list of definitions of "worry" you will find the following: "to seize (originally by the throat) with the teeth and shake or mangle, as one animal does another."

This is a graphic picture of what the worrier does to

another. For an animal to catch another by the throat with the teeth may mean death. In the many films of wildlife hunting for food in Africa, one characteristic is consistent. As soon as the predator brings down its victim, it goes for the throat. It literally chokes its victim to death. Unwittingly, persons who worry by sharing their negative outlooks literally choke off affirmative, positive, and optimistic ideas. They stifle wholesome concepts.

Worry actually chokes off physical life. This is done very gradually. Because it is a cause of death it is often not associated with worry but with the physical symptom it caused. Worry kills! It has been clinically shown how it kills. The fretting and chafing of habitual worry injures cells of the brain beyond repair. This being the message center of the body, it gradually affects other organs of the body. These diseased organs are attributed with causing death. As dropping water over a period of years gradually wears away a boulder, so worry—imperceptibly but emphatically—ever so subtly wears away the vitality of the brain.

Worry is an irritant. It is as insidious as an acid. If applied consistently, it erodes the vitality of nerve cells. Such acute cases evidence themselves by the person's becoming shaky.

The mind is like an incredibly proficient machine. If properly cared for, it can produce amazing feats. Worry hinders its miracle work.

"Sabot" is the French word for a wooden shoe. It is the root from which the word *sabotage* comes. It developed from the practice of throwing a wooden shoe into the machinery to stop its work. Worry is today's wooden shoe. When thrown into the mechanism of the mind, it sours the disposition and dispoils one's attitude. Beware of people wearing only one wooden shoe!

Further testimony as to the effect of worry has been given by Dr. W. C. Alvarez, a stomach specialist at the Mayo Clinic. He concluded that 80 percent of the stomach disorders he treats are not organic, but functional. Wrong mental attitudes and improper spiritual outlooks cause functional disturbances in the digestive system. He concludes that faith is more important than food in curing most stomach ulcers.

A smorgasbord of worry-scuttling truth is the Bible. Program your mind with its refreshing reassurances.

A compendium of concepts worth cultivating and others which merit culling is found in Psalm 37. The following extracts from that treasure trove of truth are a good starting point for readjusting your mental attitude.

> *Fret not thyself because of evildoers, neither be thou envious against the workers of iniquity. For they shall soon be cut down like the grass, and wither as the green herb. Trust in the Lord and do good; so shalt thou dwell in the land, and verily thou shalt be fed. Delight thyself also in the Lord; and he shall give thee the desires of thine heart. Commit thy way unto the Lord; trust also in him; and he shall bring it to pass . . . Rest in the Lord, and wait patiently for him: fret not thyself because of him who prospereth in his way, because of the man who bringeth wicked devices to pass. Cease from anger, and forsake wrath: fret not thyself in any wise to do evil (v. 1-5,7-8).*

Having read this passage, now go back and study it. Evaluate it. Do you believe it? If so, in applying it you will find victory over worry. A careful analysis of the passage will reveal that most of the things worried about are included as items to be excluded from your thought patterns.

Such passages as the above can afford an oasis in the desert of worry. Like a person dying of thirst in a dry, barren wasteland, drink deeply of it.

During World War II, President Harry Truman was asked, "How can you bear up so calmly under the strain and stress of the presidency?"

With typical Truman candor, he replied, "I have a foxhole in my mind. Just as a soldier retreats into his foxhole for protection and respite, I periodically retire into my mental foxhole where I allow nothing to bother me."

Each of us must have the equivalent of our own "foxhole" to survive the spiritual warfare in which we are engaged. God's Word is such a place. Get in it often!

A classic story of God's quieting a worried soul is recorded in 2 Kings 6. In verse 6, the reason for not worrying is given: "Fear not: for they that be with us are more than they that be with them."

Elisha and his manservant awoke one morning in Dothan. Both looked upon the same landscape but saw different things. As was his custom the servant arose before his master to perform his chores. Their residence in the hillside city of Dothan looked out over a wide plain. The servant was terrorized when he looked out and saw a formidable army surrounding the city. Dothan, a defenseless city, was at their mercy. Elisha, the object of the army's wrath, was without protection. This fearsome sight struck a note of alarm in the frightened servant.

The King of Syria, whose forays across Israel's borders which were assumed to be undefended, had been repetitiously frustrated by prophetic forewarning of Israel by

Elisha. In frustration, the King of Syria had sent a large expedition to capture Elisha.

A survey of the scene left the servant feeling as helpless as a person up to his armpits in alligators.

Elisha viewed the same scene but, with the eyes of faith, saw more than the servant. He beheld the angelic host of the Lord poised to defend him and defeat the Syrians. He saw in the same situation that had worried his servant a cornucopia of blessings. He had faith to see the delivering power of the Lord. Thus, his jubilant exultation, "Fear not."

Our selective perspective causes us to interpret the events of life in light of our viewpoint. Two persons looked at the same circumstance and interpreted it completely differently. One's perspective resulted in worry. The other's produced faith and its associated peace of heart.

In the early morning hours around 4 o'clock in the winter, Jupiter can be seen big and bright out our east window. This, the largest of our planets, is 484 million miles away from the sun. It is 86,000 miles in diameter. That is eleven times that of earth. One thousand three hundred (1,300) Earths would be required to fill the space occupied by Jupiter. At its closest point to Earth, it is 367,320,000 miles away. From my bedroom window a twig is bigger than Jupiter. In its orbit it passes behind a twig on a tree in our backyard. This branch is not more than two inches in diameter. Yet, it completely blocks out the planet when it passes behind it, the reason being the twig is closer to me than Jupiter. My vision is preoccupied with the closer object.

Various obstructions similarly block our spiritual vision. What we are closest to seems biggest. Focus on your worries and they seem big. Look to the Lord and worries diminish in size. He overshadows our biggest problem.

Elisha had a two-tiered faith. He saw the reality of that which was natural, but he also beheld that which was supernatural. Those not blind to their spiritual resources can "fear not."

6

Depression— Fermented Fear

Are you ever depressed?

In all honesty we each would have to admit we are given to mood swings. There are highs and lows in every life. Dr. Harold Esecover of the Columbia Psychoanalytic School noted: "I doubt that there is a person around who hasn't been touched by depression."

The National Institute of Mental Health reports that depression is a billion-dollar-a-year business. Over eight million Americans have depression deep enough to cause them to miss work or send them to the doctor.

The first known writer to categorize depression was Hippocrates, the Greek physician and philosopher. He labeled it "melancholia." He thought it was caused by heavy, black blood. In the days of Socrates it was referred to as the "black-bile" ailment. Thinking it to be a disease of the blood, depressed persons were often "bled." That is, a medical man would cut a vein and let some blood flow. This actually weakened the person with the result that depression was often intensified.

In the second century a physician, Aretaeus, described the depressed as "sad" and "dismayed." He wrote that if the state were allowed to persist, they complained of a "thousand futilities." That is still a trait of the depressed. Everything seems to go wrong. A negative air prevails.

Also writing in the second century, Plutarch observed of the depressed: "He looks on himself as a man whom the gods hate and pursue with their anger." To some who are depressed it does seem God is out to "get" them. If he were, he never would have said "fear not." Only one who wants to help would give such encouragement.

Generally speaking, there are four forms of depression. Some of these are not considered; others are. Some authorities consider all forms a symptom of a disease. In either instance, seldom is the cure simply found in telling the person to "cheer up." In most cases, there is nothing they had rather do. Often much of their frustation is that they have tried so hard to shape up.

Following is an oversimplified explanation of what happens chemically within the body to cause depression. Later the moods that activate this process in certain instances will be considered.

Your central nervous system, along with the endocrine glands, produce most of the chemicals needed for many major body functions. These chemicals regulate your hunger and sex drive and control sleep habits. In general, they make the brain function, think, and reason. Such chemicals are called hormones. An imbalance in these hormones can be produced and cause depression. One's natural body chemistry of drugs prescribed by a doctor can reverse such depression. Caution should be taken in using any mood-altering drug. As a condition initiated by depression, so an attitude change about that circumstance can reverse the process. Some degenerative phases of depression are:

A passive or listless feeling.

A feeling of sadness.

An attitude of "nothing seems good or is worth feeling good about."

A state of hopelessness fluctuates and then becomes constant.

A condition of feeling nothing ever is going to get better; there is no need trying.

A concept that no one cares; no one understands or accepts me.

A feeling that "I would be better off dead."

Finally, in the most severe cases, "I think I will kill myself."

Some or all of these are stages through which the depressed pass. Different stages are most prominent in various people.

Types of Depression

A superficial review of the four types of depression might help one determine his condition in seeking help.

Endogenous Depression is a title given one form because the cause is within the person. It is a result of a chemical imbalance in the central nervous system. Most often it is associated with some observable external cause. Symptoms include anxiety, confusion, inability to concentrate, memory loss, and a constant sad feeling. Physical symptoms include diarrhea or constipation, pressure in the chest, head, or neck, stomach pains, and dryness of mouth. The mood is worse in the morning and may appear to get better in early afternoon. Sadness prevails. Self-esteem is lost. There is an attitude of worthlessness, inferiority, guilt, and a belief that everyone despises you. Consideration of suicide is common. This is especially true if the condition is prolonged. The subject has no energy. It is even difficult for him to move at times.

Reactive Depression is so-called because it is a reaction to such things as the death or loss of a loved one or a severe personal setback. Sadness prevails and is associated with periods of anxiety. Most often there are no physical symptoms. Constant sadness reveals the mood. Self-esteem is often unaffected. A strong sense of having suffered a personal, irretrievable loss, not a self loss, exists. The energy level is normally unaffected.

Toxic Depression is caused by outside substances such as viral illness, drugs, or faulty diet. What one eats or doesn't eat is vital to this form. The symptoms are similar to those of endogenous depression. They vary from case to case and include wide mood swings. Physical symptoms are few unless there are side effects of the toxic substance. Moods range from lethargy to hyperactivity. Self-esteem varies dependent on the inducing cause. This is also true of one's energy level.

Psychotic Depression is caused by a "nervous breakdown," over-exhaustion, mental disorder, or brain disease.

Frequently, there are hallucinations and occasional manic conditions. Hypochondria causes varied physical complaints. One's behavior is unpredictable. The person is most optimistic in the morning and depressed in the evening. Self-esteem is unpredictable. The person's energy level is subject to swings from intense listlessness or wild outbursts of activity.

One of the depressing symptoms about depression is that most depressed people feel they alone are the only ones who have ever been depressed. That isn't true.

Biblical Examples

Can you imagine Moses depressed? He was a giant of a leader. His physical strength and wisdom were admirable. He was the hand by which God performed many miracles. His lips spoke the very word of God. He was alone on the mountain with God and heard his voice. Can you conceive of this man so depressed that he considered suicide? He did. This man had united the Hebrew slaves in Egypt and led them into becoming a nation contemplating suicide. This emotion is the low mark on the scale of depression. Moses, a mountain of a man, cried out to God, "I am not able to bear all these people alone . . . kill me. . . . " (Num. 11:14-15). He wanted death rather than life.

When one fears life so much that death is preferred, fear has fermented. The ingredients have soured, the substance has decayed when this low is reached.

Can you imagine Elijah depressed? In a moment of triumph he had called fire from heaven (cf. 1 Kings 18). On Mount Carmel, with God as his dependable resource, he defeated the prophets of Baal. Courageously, he defied the godless king, and queen, Ahab and Jezebel. Then when life became threatening, he desired to die. This bold man who had seen God make wet wood burn, when later pressed by a godless queen, cried out, "O Lord . . . take away my life" (1 Kings 19:4).

Can you imagine Jeremiah depressed? This prophet of God was raised from the obscurity of the little rural town of

Anathoth and instructed to confront the intelligentsia of his time. His wisdom caused wonder among the wise. He boldly proclaimed Jehovah's covenant, courageously rebuked the social sins of the day, forthrightly called on the elite to repent. Time and again God acquitted him. Yet, the Scripture records occasions when this despondent herald was so depressed he wept. He bewailed, "Oh that my head were waters, and mine eyes a fountain of tears, that I might weep day and night . . . " (Jer. 9:1). The condition of his people had depressed him. He became known as "the weeping prophet." When Jerusalem, his beloved city, was destroyed he went from bad-to-worse depression.

Can you imagine Paul depressed? He had a personal encounter with Christ on the Damascus road that transformed his life. This respected young scholar spent three years in the desert being conditioned for his role. Even the demons obeyed his voice. The intellects of Greece and Rome wondered at his wisdom. His fertile mind was sown with divine truth inspired as Scripture.

Therein, he revealed that he "despaired even of life" (2 Cor. 1:8). He became so depressed that he wanted to die more than he wanted to live. Life was tasteless. He was ready to give up. He who testified, "I can do all things through Christ which strengtheneth me" (Phil. 4:13), had to employ that strength to overcome tormenting depression. Can't you relate to that kind of person? It is encouraging to see his humanity showing. It is even more encouraging to see his victory over our common foe—depression.

Can you imagine Jonah depressed? Aftrer experiencing a miraculous deliverance from sure death, he was ensnared by this tyrant called depression. His evangelistic campaign in Nineveh was an overwhelming success. He had been an eyewitness to a unique outpouring of God's blessings on an entire city. The thrill of seeing an entire culture converted was his. Soon thereafter he was heard to implore, "O Lord, take, I beseech thee, my life . . . " (Jon. 4:3). Again one of our champions pled for death in the pit of depression.

John the Baptist! Depressed? Surely not. Yes, even this New Testament prototype of a loyalist to our Lord was found drearily depressed in a dungeon, even to the extent that he began to doubt Jesus' Messiahship.

Abraham in Canaan when the famine came, Moses at Meribah when there was no water, Job scraping his skin ulcers, and Peter locked in an upper room attest to the generality of depression.

Abraham Lincoln, who sought to unite a nation, found his own self divided within and depressed. Temperamentally, he tended toward depression.

We need ever to be mindful that our bodies are heirs to a variety of weaknesses. Our heritage does not control us, but it does influence us. Observe your relatives. Are they prone to depression? This gives you no excuse to follow their pattern, but it may help you avoid doing so out of habit. Know your nature. Don't let it master you. Instead let it serve you. Control it—don't let it control you.

Sir Winston Churchill was a courageous clarion voice who repeatedly called the Allied nations of World War II back from the brink of collective depression. He himself was so hounded by depression that he referred to it as a "black dog." He tended to give it personality, it was so real to him. The conditions of the world bore down on him and caused him depression even as he exhorted others.

Study your conditions. Know the pressure put on you and respond energetically.

Americans heralded the phenomenal feat of "Buzz" Aldrin as he soared to the heights of the moon. Soon after his return to earth he plummeted into deep depression. It was feared he might never regain his sanity. His environment had brought stress on him like few have ever known. Analyze your environment. Know the factors therein that create stress and that tend toward your being depressive.

England listened and the world read with ebullient joy the preaching of Charles H. Spurgeon. He was a man of wit and warmth. This sage suffered depression brought on by painful and eventually fatal gout. At a modestly young age he died of this disease which manifested itself in his big toe. He not only died of a toeache, he suffered depression because of it. Know your health. There are physical factors which can weaken you and create conditions conducive for depression.

David, the sweet singer of Israel, was deprived of a place of worship, and depression developed. Worship is a therapy which wards off depression. Include it in your weekly schedule.

When things change in our lives, conditions often become uncertain. As good things move out of our lives or bad things move in, we often become uncertain. Disappointment, helplessness, and frustration are frequent feelings which accompany that which is new and unfamiliar. Death, rejection, reversals, omission, or disappointments can cause that "down" feeling. They can serve as the roots from which irritability, criticism, pessimism, and indecisiveness grow. When these moods develop and nothing seems to be fun, the depression skid has begun.

Uncertain events of circumstances serve as a brewery

where fear works as the yeast of fermentation, producing depression.

Depression is not always a disease. It is often a symptom. Two general categories of fear-fermenting factors exist. One is constitutional.

Our physical makeup. Again we should remind ourselves not to let this become an excuse for undue fits of depression.

The second is environment. This one is more diversified. It encompasses all the stress factors to which we are subject. These factors cause mood swings between elation and gloom. The latter sometimes comes as the "blahs." It progresses to the "blues." When it further decays, it is more like the "black indigos."

Isaiah called depression "the spirit of heaviness" (61:3). It may come in the form of mild or intense apathy, pessimism, grief, sadness, guilt, self-condemnation, or lethargy. Frequent physical traits are a loss of appetite, restlessness, insomnia, intemperance, and, in acute cases, thoughts of suicide.

Fear is the catalyst which causes this bitter brew to ferment. Therefore, an emotional preservative must be mixed with the uncertain events of life to avoid depression.

Centuries ago the prophet, Haggai, addressed his uncertain generation and reminded them of that which is worthy of our recall. God had promised, "My Spirit remaineth among you, fear ye not" (2:5). He offered an antidote along with a sweet incentive.

Before considering the three-fold bromide, let's review the circumstances. The Lord had moved in the heart of Cyrus, king of Persia, and motivated him to allow the return of a Jewish remnant from Babylonian captivity to their native land. Their commendable zeal for national restoration was curtailed by political intrigue. Work on the Temple stopped. Their new-born enthusiasm was short-lived in light of their prolonged problems. Only Zerubbabel and Joshua survived and served as twin lamps to reignite their zestful efforts. The dismayed mass had become more concerned about their own comforts than about the reconstruction of the house of the Lord. The paralysis of depression smothered all initiative. Work ceased.

An elixir from the Lord was soon administered by Haggai. In concentrated form, it was "fear not."

Upon hearing it, they could have replied, "You don't understand. Ours is a peculiar situation. We are defenseless, feeble, and our enemies are formidable. God, if you know what we know, you would be afraid also."

Spiritual Reassurance

Three ingredients composed this tonic labeled "fear not."

First, the pledge of the Lord. He promised, "My Spirit remaineth among you. . . ."

The writer of Hebrews referred to Jesus Christ as the "forerunner" of believers (6:20). The Greek word translated forerunner is *prodromos*. It was a word used to identify a pilot who knew a home port better than any sea captain. When the ship was about to enter the port, the pilot would go on board and take charge. He knew the channels and was best able to guide it safely to its dock.

That is what the Lord wants to do in our lives. We are not alone. He is with us to guide us. There may be times when you do not feel like he is with you; the fact is, he is. Regardless of our feelings, he has said, "I will never leave thee, nor forsake thee." He has promised to be with us "even unto the end of the world." Claim those promises. Acknowledge his presence. It might even help to admit to him you do not feel like he is present. Having done so, then acknowledge your gratitude for the fact of his presence even without the feeling. In this way, faith is given occasion to walk on its own two feet without sight. As a result, faith gains strength.

On one of the many times when King David was attempting a recovery from depression, he employed three steps as revealed in Psalm 42.

He first made an *admission.* He admitted his depression. "Why art thou cast down?" He faced the fact and admitted it. He did not try piously to pretend that his kind never felt "down." He did not go through great analytical efforts trying to excuse it or ignore it.

He admitted he felt God had forsaken and asked, "Why hast thou forgotten me?" God had not, but David felt he had. Have you ever felt that way? If you have, you are not alone. Admit it. That is a vital expenditure of energy in the recovery process. God will not get mad with you. He understands and still loves you. It is his nature, not your goodness, that prompts him to love you. Your goodness may vary; his nature does not.

Hope is not a tenant in a heart that has never been broken. It resides in those broken and healed. Like the pure, bright light from a star, it reaches the uplifted eye of the hopeful pilgrim to inspire and renew. Hope begins a new emergence with its healing effect when one admits his plight. There are only two places where hope is not existent: heaven and hell. It is fulfilled in heaven and impossible in hell. Let it begin its bud emergence by admitting your depression. Twice on this occasion David cried out, "Hope thou in God."

This open candor with the Lord shows trust in him. It is the first move toward admitting a desire to experience an awareness of his presence.

He next made an *affirmation*. He affirmed that God had been with him and blessed him. A person may awaken in the morning and not feel married, although he is married. Later in the day an attractive member of the opposite sex strolls along. There may be a social and physical attraction between the two. Soon the person who does not feel married may begin to act as though he is not married. The potentially disastrous result this can cause can be averted if the person not feeling married were to affirm, "I am married." Action follows affirmation. By self-affirming the state of marriage, appropriate action is more likely to follow.

David's affirmation was spurred on by remembering what the Lord had done for him. Many people find reading from the Psalms to be inspirational. A careful analysis will reveal that in writing many of them David was in a state of depression. He rapidly moved from acknowledging it to praising and thanking the Lord for his goodness. This elevated David emotionally. It lifted him from defeating depression.

In yet another Psalm, David reminds us, "Many are the afflictions of the righteous; but the Lord delivereth them out of them" (34:19).

The ancient Roman, Horace, spoke of the value of trials:

> *Difficulties elicit talents that in more fortunate circumstances would lie dormant.*

Former British Prime Minister Disraeli concurred: "Difficulties constitute the best education in this life."

If we will but pause and reflect, we can see how lovingly our Lord has worked us through many difficulties. He often actually changes them into blessings. It helps to affirm that the Lord has been with us and seen us through crisis. His comforting words "fear not" have often been the justifiable stabilizer in moments of need.

Finally, he made an *attestation*. He attested that his very existence was summed up in God. He exalted, "God is my life." God is bigger than a broken arm, bigger than a divorce, a lost athletic contest, a missed business deal, a death, or a financial reversal. He is bigger than our biggest need. Fear not!

Secondly, he attested that God was stable. He proclaimed, "God is my rock." Rocks don't shift positions. In this uncertain world, some stable footing is needed. God is thus depicted as being supportive.

In the Bible lands, rocks are often used as landmarks. They serve very much like roadsigns in the desert. Each rock marks a particular place and gives directions. When one can say, "God is my rock," he is acknowledging he knows where he is and where he is going. God is that reassuring pillar reminding us to "fear not."

The second ingredient Haggai offered on behalf of the Lord, as a component in the "fear-not" tonic, is an exhortation: "Be strong." This is a reference to the power of the Lord. Their strength was derived from the presence of the Lord. They had already sufficiently demonstrated their own weakness of character and commitment. An awareness that his spirit remained among them as an ally caused them to "fear not."

Much depression is caused by a state of mind. It is

essential to work to change such a mind. Certain forms of depression need to be treated clinically. Some are aided dietetically. In instances of persistent depression, medical help should be sought. There are, however, certain basic steps one can take, often effective, in breaking the spell of depression. These should be employed.

The apostle Paul encouraged the fear-riddled Ephesians with words applicable to us: "Be strong in the Lord, and in the power of his might" (Eph. 6:10).

On an athletic team each player is made stronger by the strongest. The greater the ability of a superstar, the better the team. The strength is in union. Remember to rely on your union with the Lord. Let his strength be yours. Consciously reflect upon Bible truths that feed your mind thoughts of his strength. Soak your mind with such truths. Recall historical events which evidence his ability to help the helpless.

Also, think through some of your own past victories. Honestly assess God's role in previous events that enabled you to be an overcomer. Don't hide behind false modesty. Admit God has blessed you and afforded you help in times past. If you find nothing current for which to praise him, use these previous blessings as something for which to thank him currently. Likely you did not do an adequate job of thanking him in the first place. There is strength in a thankful heart. Praise him!

Isaiah wisely prescribed an antidote, "Produce your cause, bring forth your strong reasons . . . " (41:21). Analytically, do it!

This is an encouragement to use logic and reason. Clear your mind of fantasy. That is what Paul meant by "pulling down of strong holds." In the following verse he spoke about "casting down imaginations" (2 Cor. 10:4-5). Don't fantasize. The mind can run away. The Philippian Christians of the New Testament were the first to receive the letter which urges us to be "in nothing terrified by your adversary" (Phil. 1:28). The Greek word translated "terrified" was used to describe a horse, "spooked" in battle, that had run away. That is a graphic description of what can happen in one's mind. Don't let it panic and run away with fantasized negative thoughts.

State your "case." That is, face reality, good or bad; it is easier to deal with that than vain imagination. It can never be dealt with constructively as long as you are playing mental games. Therefore, do everything you can rationally to line up reality and give it a thorough inspection. That is a first step to recovery. Don't be pretentious. Things may be very bad, but they are seldom as bad as we imagine them to be.

Joshua listed a reliable companion of strength: "Be strong and of good courage; be not afraid, neither be thou dismayed; for the Lord thy God is with thee whithersoever thou goest" (Josh. 1:9). The same theme emerges here again—in the presence of the Lord there is strength. He is with you. Acknowledge it as a fact and act accordingly.

As a deep-sea diver is dependent upon his diving gear, so we are dependent upon the Lord. One is made stronger by wearing one's gear. Without it one is helpless. The believer is "in the Lord." In a hostile environment he adapts us for survival. Envision yourself enveloped in God's great love, overshadowed by his presence, enabled by his strength.

The third ingredient Haggai offered was instruction to "work." This is the proposal of the Lord.

By service you can have a significant and successful life.

The determining factor is not the past, but your hope for the future. A sense of destiny is more important than past history or present entanglement. A sad saint is a sad sort of saint. A servicing saint is a satisfied saint. An awareness that the Lord is with you as you serve gives the capacity to say, "Yes or no—and whoopee."

Wendell Willkie, candidate for president in 1940, once asked Franklin Roosevelt, "Why do you keep that frail, sickly Harry Hopkins at your elbow?" President Roosevelt answered, "Hundreds come through that door daily who want something from me. Harry Hopkins wants only to serve me. That is why he is so near to me." Service brings us close to the Lord.

Dostoevski noted, "The ant knows the formula for the anthill. The bee knows the formula for the beehive. They do not know the formulae in a human way, but in their own way. Only man does not know his formula."

If we do not, it is because of willful ignorance. "Work" is the most elementary part of our formula. "Serve the Lord with gladness." Gladness comes from serving the Lord.

Physical Responses

While continuing to employ such mental/spiritual therapy, it is also wise to take certain practical steps to compensate for some of the physical influences of depression. Try these:

- *Spend as much time in bed as you normally do. Don't spend more than usual. Even if you can't sleep, still spend the time in bed. Some rest will result.*
- *Eat adequately. If the appetite has been killed, eat*

five small meals a day. This will keep the caloric intake down but the important blood sugar available.

- *Spend some time alone. Don't overdo it. Do allow yourself adequate quiet time to employ the aforementioned attitudinal therapy.*
- *Do something fun. It may seem all the fun has gone out of life. Force some back in. You may not feel like it, but do it. Thus, an external, favorable force is bringing influence on unfavorable, internal ones. Fun is OK.*
- *Do something strenuous. If you have had a medical check-up and know it is all right to engage in strenuous pursuits, do it. Energy solicits and generates energy. This can help your energy flow.*
- *Do something social. Again, you may not feel like it. That is the reason why you should do it. It, too, is OK. By doing so, you will be moving into a positive environment which can have a very positive emotional influence. Drive yourself to do it. It can be fun. Relax and try to let people lift your spirit. Don't feel obligated to try to pull them down into your temporary pit. They might not know how to get out.*
- *Do something spiritual. It is not wise automatically to assume your problem is spiritually induced. Don't overlook the possibility, either. Engagement in a positive worship experience is therapeutic. It can unshackle your spirit and let it soar.*

Some persons want to withdraw and think. Often it is said, "I can understand God's will if I can just get away and think." Some of that is good. However, there is a better way. Solomon's wisdom was never more practical than when he wrote: "Commit thy works unto the Lord, and thy thoughts shall be established" (Prov. 16:3).

To find the unknown, start with the known. Do what you know you should do, and the unknown will be revealed. Once more reread the steps just suggested. They are now some things you know you should do. Take them one by one and commit the doing of them to the Lord. In the process of doing them, you likely will find relief. Do what you know you should do. Do it even if you emotionally don't feel like doing it. Don't let your emotions control your doing. Let your doing help control your emotions.

Now a word of caution. Don't overdo. The body slows down when it is physically ill. It instinctively does so to allow for energy reserves to be used to throw off the illness. Behind this reflexively imposed curtain, work goes on to repair the body. Some of the slowdown associated with depression is for the same purpose. In urging persons not to overdo, they must also be reminded not to use this as an excuse not to do at all. Balance is a key factor.

When depressed, the mind tends to go around in circles. Activities must be engaged, and that will break it out of this pattern. Proper engagements can help put it back on the straight and narrow.

7

Anxiety—
Frustrated Fear

Before a word could be spoken, Jane sat speechless, her lips pursed as if restraining breath itself. When her emotions were controlled enough for her to talk, she shared for the first time events that had wrecked her life. Physical evidences of what her tormenting thought had done were evident. She had lost much weight, could not maintain her job, was unable to sleep, shook like a vibrating, loose guitar string, and spoke almost incoherently. Such outward evidences marked her life as one filled with anxiety.

Two dramatic events had driven her worst fears underground in her thoughts. Three years earlier she had a baby out of wedlock. One year before our counseling session, she had married a man who accepted her and the baby as they were. On Christmas Day, about six months after marriage, he shot himself.

In her own crass way, she asked, "Can a bastard baby go to heaven?" Secondly, she sobbed, "Can a person who kills himself go to heaven? I've been told the Bible says they can't."

After I explained the true biblical insight into these two difficult issues, she smiled slightly. Relief had begun. Further conversation helped her to understand that one's eternal destiny is dependent on his acceptance or rejection of Jesus

Christ as Savior, not his manner of conception or death. Tension was dissipated. Her recovery had begun. Her anxiety had been defused by facts.

There is a slight but significant difference in anxiety and worry. Anxiety is, according to its derivation, a choking disquieting, which is akin to anguish. Worry is more petty, restless, and manifest. Anxiety is most often quiet or silent; worry is usually communicated to all around. Worry and anxiety grow from the same seed. Worry grows up like the stalk of a weed. It is visible and expressive. Anxiety grows down into the mind like the root of a plant. If uncontrolled, the root system spreads. Such a root system chokes off all fertile thought. Anxiety fields its substance in painful events of the past. Its occasion is some weakness in the present. All joy is replaced by anxiety. It leaves life sterile. Spontaneity is stripped from a life because of anxiety, or uncertain feeling, about the future.

An old map of Jamaica shows a territory marked "the land of looking behind." It dates back to the time when the cruel and inhuman practice of slavery was common. When slaves escaped they would head for the mountains. Government troops were sent out to recapture these poor runaways. A fleeing slave spent much time looking back. From this came the designation of the region.

Even when such a runaway escaped from the sugar plantation, he was not free. They were slaves to fear. One taskmaster of fear is named anxiety.

Anxiety is frustrated fear.

Jane was frustrated not only because of her lack of truthful insight, but by her misinformation. Persons whom she trusted had told her certain things were in the Bible regarding her two sources of anxiety. In truth, the alleged Bible quotes she had been fed were not at all in the

Scriptures. Her anxiety could have been caused by Bible ignorance alone. It was, however, made more complex by misinformation. Truth is imperative to the conquest of anxiety.

Anxiety is the fear of which Coleridge spoke in *The Rime of the Ancient Mariner*:

> *Fear at my heart, as at a cup,*
> *My life-blood seemed to sip!*

It drains one's mental bank, energy reserve, and emotional strength. Once these assets are drained, the subject is vulnerable to attack by less formidable forces. Otherwise, these weaker attitudinal assailants would easily be defeated. A depleted state of mind can't handle even the least fear factor.

Physical Impact

Anxiety as an emotion has a profound influence on the body. A division of the body's entire nervous system is called the "sympathetic nervous system." This system is responsible for the physical signs associated with acute or chronic anxiety. It is activated by two chemicals secreted by the adrenal glands. The sympathetic nervous system is important in maintaining the integral functioning of the many organ systems of the body. When anxiety arises, the sympathetic nerves to the intestines cause them to temporarily slow down or stop digestive action. A result is the familiar "knot" in the stomach. Other physical traits associated with an anxiety attack are: cold skin, sweaty, dilated pupils; a fine, fast tremor in the hands, an increased heartbeat, slowed digestion and increased breathing. There is a tendency to nausea or vomiting and diarrhea. The stomach may be constantly upset or "in a knot."

Progression to anxiety goes as follows. First, there is psychological or physical stress. Fear is created. It rapidly deteriorates into worry. It becomes repressed as anxiety.

The speed with which this type of anxiety develops is influenced by the nature of the stress. It may be almost instantaneous. Frequently, it builds over a period of time. It can be dispelled rapidly as a crisis is passed or be maintained for a prolonged period if not constructively handled.

The causes of anxiety seem to outlive their victims. For example, note these quoted conditions. "The world has grown old and lost its vigor; the mountains are gutted, the mines are exhausted, the fields lack farmers."

If history had a personality it would be smiling at those made anxious by that report. Though modern reports and pundits make a living by parroting virtually those same statements, they were actually authored by Saint Cyprian over 1,700 years ago.

Some things, though unworthy of our attention and concern, solicit our anxiety. Ageless problems still produce perplexities today. Their very antiquity should cause us to dispel them as unworthy of our fretful care. Ageless anxieties walk the corridors of modern minds. Their intrepid step is still quick and spry. Age has not diminished their vitality. Not even our sophisticated, contemporary enlightenment has banished many of our oldest anxiety adversaries.

Attitude Makes the Difference

It was said of Omar Khayyam: "He spent his whole life in the cellar and thought it was the only room in the house." Anxiety is a cellar dweller's paradise. Without new thought to ventilate the mind it remains locked in the basement of anxiety. Relief results when one dares to venture into the sunlight of affirmative, positive, creative thought.

Andrew Carnegie observed, "The power of thought is the only thing over which any human being has complete control."

People, places, and things are outside influences bringing pressure on every life. Most lives are subject to about the same bombardment as others. Some capitulate while others conquer under the same siege. What makes the difference? Attitude! That should cause a thrill. It means you can triumph. After all, Mr. Carnegie observed that is the only thing over which you have absolute control. No matter what happens externally *you and you alone* have control over your reaction. You are in the final sense responsible. Quit blaming others and acknowledge that your attitude put you here. By changing you can overcome even the most imposing externals.

The Bible is a service manual for dealing with anxiety. When the thoughts contained therein are transferred to one's mind, that mind is controlled by peace-producing principles.

Christ spoke of his dear friend, Martha, as being "careful [anxious] . . . about many things" (Luke 10:41). His instructions are that we should be "careful [anxious] for nothing."

Philippians 4:6-9 is a case book for dealing with anxiety. To try to deny the spiritual aspect of life and deal correctly with trying issues is foolish. It is as unwise as it would be for an amateur boxer, with one hand tied behind him and a patch covering one eye, to climb into a ring with a world-class fighter. We appreciably handicap ourselves when we fail to use spiritual assets.

With the church at Philippi serving as a model, we are instructed that we should "be careful for nothing." This translates *meden merimnate,* which is a present imperative meaning "you be anxious about nothing," or literally "stop being anxiety-ridden." The Green terminology means to be torn apart. Anxiety tears our minds away from those things which serve as its antidote. It divides the mind, separating it from stabilizing principles. In this condition one is divided from reasoning and recovery resources. Thus, anxiety becomes the accrued interest we pay in advance on the debt of unbelief with which we mortgage life.

How to Deal with Anxiety

The Philippian passage serves as a how-to kit for dealing with anxiety.

Step one—Don't be full of care; be full of prayer.

In a 1920 edition of the *Yale Review,* H. L. Mencken noted, "The one permanent emotion of the inferior man, as of all simple mammals, is fear—fear of the unknown, the complex, and the inexplicable."

Among human beings this universal trait should serve as a stimuli for prayer.

Proseuche is the Greek word translated prayer. It involves more than simply "saying a prayer." It is a general term speaking of devotion and worship. Talking to the Lord is a part of it. Encompassed therein, however, is the sum total of one's devotional life. One willfully worships God when God's nature is considered. He is good. It is his nature. He can't be otherwise. He is loving. It is his essence. He can't be otherwise. This kind of God is deserving of our devotion.

The story is told of an East Coast fishing village in destitute conditions. Townspeople decided to hold a meeting, trying to resolve their complicated problems. It was attended by a stranger who tried several times to speak. There being a bit of community prejudice, the visitor was interrupted each time he tried. The local townspeople didn't care for an outsider to become involved. A latecomer to the meeting saw the visitor leave early and asked, "What was he doing here? Did he offer help? Is he going to aid us?" Members of the unknowing assembly asked who he was. The latecomer replied, "I saw his boat docked in the harbor. That was John D. Rockefeller, Sr., who had come to offer his help."

As the helpful resources of our God exceed those of Rockefeller, so our intemperate rudeness exceeds that of the villagers. We must begin by realizing our God who wants to help us *can help us*. He is deserving of our devotion and worship. True worship is therapeutic. Try it and you will see.

A watch may lack only one thing—a *main spring*; a car only one thing—a *carburetor*; a body one thing—life. Without these parts the whole is incomplete. If the one thing lacking in a life is devotion and worship, that life is missing life's inoculation against anxiety.

There is an often-told story of a student who lived a reckless life destined for trouble. There was only one person in his life who received his respect. The student was loved by a teacher who demonstrated true compassion for him. Ultimately, the student responded in three phases.

He came to accept the teacher as his teacher.

He learned from her what was right.

He loved her so much that he wanted to do what was right.

Every person needs to take those attitudes as his own in relation to the Lord. Each is a prelude to the other. The ultimate act of love educates us about how to be emancipated from anxiety. Anxiety is a chloroform as subtle and deadly as gases used in chemical warfare. It divides our mind, separating us from Christ. If not overcome, it will overcome us.

Step two in dealing with anxiety involves making special petitions known to God. In the Philippian letter this is called "supplication." In this process one pauses to make known to the Lord his requests. That is generally called prayer, though it is a type of prayer called supplication. It is asking for the Lord to supply a need.

In such prayers, remember it is a request, not a dictate. When prayer is understood to be a request and not a mandate then *no* can be appreciated as a vital answer. When a child makes a request of a loving parent, *no* is a viable answer. Somewhere we have become confused in thinking the only answer to prayer is *yes.* Often because of superior wisdom and love, a parent refuses a child's request. In such a case it is the loving thing to do. Our Heavenly Father is no less loving and much more knowledgeable. He, too, reserves the right to a *no.*

In light of his love, knowledge, and sense of humor, God might well give one of three responses:

"Yes!"

"No!"

"You've got to be kidding!"

When God is asked to supply a need, he takes that request into consideration. His response is based on superior love and knowledge. Once the request is made, there is cause for relaxation on behalf of the pray-er. The supply will either be granted or denied. If it is given, the need will be met. If it is not granted, it is because what was requested was not best for us. In either case we should rejoice and relax. In the latter case an opportunity has been given to further explore God's will and ask for that which is rightly needed. He always hears and answers.

Emotional release is possible by realizing that, by utilizing the principle of supplication, you have called upon the ultimate source to supply your need. Having done the optimum, now relax. Anxiety brews when allowed to remain unexpressed. Even if you feel you can't express the cause of anxiety even to your best friend, you can express it to God. In doing it there is gained a different perspective. Hope is reborn. Despair is dissipated. Ambition is aroused. Expectation is awakened.

Often we pray cosmetically. We want only the superficial to be changed. Change must come at the source.

There was an old-timer who frequently responded to the invitation in his church and was heard to pray, "Lord, clean out the cobwebs!" That was a great prayer. The trouble was he prayed it often with no apparent change in his reprobate life-style. On one such occasion of response, his wife was overheard to pray, "Lord, never mind the cobwebs, just kill the spiders."

In asking the Lord to supply your needs, be careful in identifying them. In prayer, you can get down to the basic nitty and fundamental gritty with God.

Don't profess the Lord to be your Shepherd and then try to pull the wool over his eyes.

Prince Potemkin, Catherine the Great's paramour and prime minister of Russia, performed one of the most impressive wool-pulling feats in history. For years the Russian empress supplied him with money to build new settlements in Siberia. He pocketed the money and professed the building. He never got around to any construction. Catherine, confined to her royal routine, never knew she was fooled. Unexpectedly, she announced she wanted to see one of her new towns. Potemkin ordered a staged-prop village with lavish exteriors but nothing be built inside. The empress toured the village without emerging from her carriage. She was completely fooled by the facade.

A pretentious life can be deceptive even to the closest of friends. God sees behind the facade. Don't try to play tricky, deceptive games with him. Tell him of your innermost need. Represent reality as it is. He already knows. He just wants to hear it from you. In this manner he knows you know. That is the beginning of release from anxiety-causing pretense.

You can even pray with the Hoosier poet, James Whitcomb Riley:

> Bring unto the sorrowing all release from pain,
> Let the lips of laughter overflow again.

Step three in dealing with anxiety is thanksgiving. Prayer and petitions must be mingled with praise.

Praise him for his ability to alleviate anxiety. Consider this capsule insight into his power. On the occasion of his crucifixion Jesus said he could call 72,000 angels. That enormous angelic resource was available to him. The number of Passover lambs listed as slain in an ancient inventory, multiplied by the number required to eat each lamb, indicates that there were approximately 250,000 people in Jerusalem at the time of the crucifixion. All of those were not enemies of Christ, but suppose that number favored his execution. So, 72,000 to 250,000 put Christ in a superior position when it is recalled that in the Old Testament one angel is reported to have killed 185,000 Assyrian warriors. At Calvary, Jesus had at his disposal a kill power of 13,320,000,000. Even that is a pittance when compared with his summary exaltation,

"All power is given unto me in heaven and in earth" (Matt. 28:18).

Thank God, he has the ability to meet your greatest need. No cause of anxiety is too weighty for him. Trust him. He doesn't abuse or misuse his power.

Thank God, he cares. The late British writer, George MacDonald, in *Robert Falconer* shared three reasons for thanksgiving instead of anxiety. "This is a sane, wholesome, practical, working faith: first, that it is a man's business to do the will of God; second, that God takes on Himself the special care of that man; third, therefore, that man ought never to be afraid of anything."

Review that line of logic. Thank God for caring.

The God of origins is the God of endings. He was in control when the world began, and he will be when it ends. In the interim his control in your life is optional. It is up to you. A mind fixed on him is stable and secure. A mind divided is the breeding ground for anxiety.

Life is more dynamic when thanksgiving and *thanksliving* are incorporated. When you awake in the morning, thank God you were born. Think of all the good things you would have missed if you had never been born.

In the Anglo-Saxon language, the word "thankful" was spelled thinkful. When we pause and think, we have cause to be thankful. Attitude makes the difference. An ancient skeptic wrote: "The things that only make me curse cause them to praise their God." Gratitude affects your attitude. True thanksgiving is a spirit, an attitude, not dependent on substance or abundance.

Most of us live in a house large enough to house many nightmares. They are ably ridden by anxiety. They must be bridled. The bit is thanksgiving.

Thanksgiving turns trials into blessings.

It releases faith on the wings of gratitude.

It will transform your inner being.

It will produce a new and more attractive personality.

It will assure that you are giving God the glory he deserves.

It recognizes the Lord is God. Thanksgiving is *to* someone not just *for* something. With this realization, one can thank God even when things are not going well.

Thanksgiving is a reaction of joy. Thanks is verbal. Giving is visual. A doctor does not determine a patient's health by his speech but by his pulse. Likewise, God doesn't simply go by our words but our lives. To live thanks is to give thanks.

Thanksgiving and praise take us beyond the boundary of reason. There is no ultimate number. So, always standing at the end of the road of reason is a question mark. Thanksgiving straightens it into an exclamation mark.

Our thanks to God is not for his good but "for *he is* good." Fire is hot, water is wet, ice is cold: it is their nature. God is good: it is his nature.

A word of thanksgiving or a song of praise can unlock the prison of anxiety.

The virtue of thanksgiving gives victory over frustrated fear—anxiety.

A spirit of thanklessness makes the heart nervous and neurotic. It eats the soul out of one's personality and makes that person a torture to self and a torment to others.

Many psychologists believe a person's emotions are controlled by conditions around him. Though conditions and circumstances are influential, they are not the controlling factors. A bee finds nectar in the same flower from which a spider gains its substance for poison.

Osmosis is a chemical process whereby substance in a greater concentration seeps into one of lesser concentration. For example, take an aquarium divided by a very porous substance. In one side is placed distilled water—in the other, water with a high concentration of salt. Soon the greater concentration will seep through the divider and taint the pure water. The solution of lesser concentration never moves into the greater.

Our attitude is the membrane separating our state of mind from circumstances. If within us there is a strong will, an optimistic outlook, a spirit of hope, and an attitude of trust, no outside concentration can seep in and control our attitude. Conversely, our attitude will permeate all around us. The ability is within you. Anxiety can be abated.

The Philippian panacea for anxiety uses two indefinite pronouns to contrast opposites—"nothing" and "everything" (4:6). They are mutually exclusive. Those who pray about everything will be anxious about nothing.

When this approach is taken, God's peace keeps the heart-attitude. It serves as a garrison. When we dwell on our problems, we go to pieces. When we dwell on Christ, we have peace. The option rests in attitude. With one's own free will, the choice is made.

Program Your Mind

The Philippian penman, having written what we must rid our minds of (namely anxiety) now asserts the replacement thoughts. Six adjectives are employed to define a mental sanctuary from anxiety. These are things on which the mind should concentrate. "Think" on these.

The Greek word for think carries the idea of reasoning through a matter logically and carefully. Elsewhere in the

New Testament it is translated variously as "account," "reckon," "reason," or "conclude." It refers not to casual thought but to serious thinking.

True = (Greek, *alethes*). Avoid plastic, phony thinking. Deal with fact, not fantasy. Relate to what is real and reliable. If the mind is divided or diverted by dwelling on figments of the imagination, it can't dwell on Bible truths. A battle goes on between these two mind-sets. You willfully determine which prevails.

Honest = (Greek, *dikaios*). Dwell on what is right and righteous. Strive to maintain the loftiest attitude of what is right. Avoid the base and debasing. Give to God and people what is right. An honest attitude is duty faced and duty done. Always think the best of every person and situation.

Pure = (Greek, *hagnos*). When this word was used ceremonially regarding Jewish worship, it meant that which had been cleansed and made fit to be brought before God. When used of one's attitude, it means not to have thoughts mixed with what debases the spirit. Pure thoughts are thoughts purged of anxiety. Distill your unclean concepts.

Lovely = (Greek, *prosphiles*). Such thoughts replace ugly and arrogant attitudes. Gracious, morally attractive ones that inspire the soul must prevail. Such an outlook brings forth love. A mind-set of kindness, sympathy, forbearance, and love makes the Christian winsome. Gracious is a synonym for such an attitude. It is antithetical to anxiety which is graceless.

Good Report = (Greek, *euphemos*). One should think and speak only those things good for people and God to hear. Well-spoken, good-sounding truths are utterances evidencing a good attitude. By hearing and speaking them, the mind is bombarded from two directions by anxiety-quieting principles.

Virtue = (Greek, *arete*). In classical use it referred to any kind of excellence: architectural, athletic, artistic, and the like. Excellence is the essence. Defeatist, pessimistic, negative, looser attitudes are stifled by virtuous concepts. Elevate your attitude. It can't be done by dwelling on that which is base.

Praise = (Greek, *epainos*). We are challenged to dwell on things that are praiseworthy. Personally, we should never conceitedly desire it or foolishly despise it. There is not room for a critical nature to breathe when a complimentary praise nature is in residence.

The text is summarized by an exhortation to "think on these"—*(logidzesthe)*. This is an appeal carefully to reflect on such subjects. It is encouragement to fill your mind with these things which give contentment and meaning to life. Think them through logically and clearly. By flooding your mind with these outlooks, you drown anxiety. When a deep freeze is filled with lean, fresh meat and vegetables, there is no room for the garbage. A mind preoccupied with these concepts is not divided by anxiety—producing ideas.

In concluding this poignant Philippian passage, the apostle Paul inserts one further directive. It goes beyond mean attitude and involves action. That word is "do." Outlook determines outcome. With the right mental perspective one can become a doer.

I have a two-word motto in my desk. It is compressed dynamite. Everytime I open the drawer there it is challenging me. It states simply—"DO IT." That is the only way mountains are moved. It is the only way you remove your covers in the morning. It is the activist's axiom, the mover's motivation, the doer's directive—DO IT.

Somewhere years ago I encountered a verse which became framed in my mind.

He dined beneath the moon
He basked beneath the sun,
He lives a life of "going to do,"
And died with nothing done.

"Do" (Greek, *prassete*) means practice. The things just mentioned are not to be strung as beads of wisdom on the cord of thought and used ornamentally. They are to leave the incubator of ideals and walk as mature actions. These principles have not been inventoried simply to allow persons to accumulate academic facts. They are imperatives. They must be done if anxiety is to be overcome. Just knowing them and not employing them can create worse anxiety.

Take them one at a time. Think of it every day of the week. Resolve to let it become characteristic of your life. Dwell on only one the first week. The second week move on to the next. Consciously try to let it become a trait of your life. Each week review those of the previous weeks and add another. In this manner it is easier to let one become entrenched before assuming the challenge of another. Such a gradual but sure conversion of concept can change your total perspective of life. Anxiety is thus deflated like a balloon.

In the realm of chemistry there is a difference in a mixture and a compound. Iron filings and sulphur can be mixed to form a compound. They can easily be separated with a magnet. If these same two substances are mixed and properly heated, they become a compound, ferrous sulfide.

The elements of attitude justly advocated can be memorized as principles and merely serve as a mixture in life, if not applied. If the circumstances of life are allowed to provide heat and they are lived out in a crucible of crisis, a compound is formed. They become personality traits. It is these traits which can overcome or prevent anxiety.

"Fear not." Stop fear. Don't let frustrated fear become anxiety.

A reporter for *The New York Herald* sat on a ridge overlooking a strategic battlefield at Cedar Creek. General Grant had named General Philip H. Sheridan to lead the cavalry of the Army of the Potomac in the defense of the area. "Little Phil," as he became known, was eleven miles away in Winchester when the battle broke out at Cedar Creek. Observing what appeared to be a rout by the Confederates, the reporter wrote, "I am witnessing the awful destruction of the United States of America." Sheridan rode at a gallop the full eleven miles to the contest. As he rode onto the field of battle, he had at his side a simple banner with a star thereon signifying his command. As he rode, he shouted, "Here is Sheridan. Sheridan is with you. Follow me and we will save the Union." They did—both.

As you do battle with your adversary, anxiety, it will help if you rephrase Sheridan: "Jesus is here. Jesus is with me. By following him he will save me from my anxiety."

Only as Sheridan's troops obeyed his command were they successful. His presence was of inspiring and helpful importance, but their positive response was also essential. Christ is with you. That presence is imperative for overcoming fear. However, you must willfully, mentally respond to his lead. You must obey his authoritative orders.

Act in direct conflict with your usual area of anxiety. Do it. Don't do it alone. The Lord has already given the order, "Fear not." Now in direct obedience to his command, act. Realize that you are not acting alone and that you are under orders. Rely on the resources of your Commander.

Don't feel bound by human nature. It is not something that is etched in stone. It is something that is always in the process of becoming. Let your nature continue to be conformed to the image of Jesus Christ. As a developing person, life remains exciting with habitual, new frontiers and perpetual conquests. The excitement does not fade.

If you feel it is your nature to be filled with anxiety, you are trapped. Discard this incorrect attitude. Flex your mental muscles and acknowledge you are more than habit. You are a vibrant, growing, unique human being with a will that can overcome even your most dread anxiety.

Goethe beautifully described two mutually exclusive elements in life:

> *We always hope; and*
> *in all things it is*
> *   better to hope*
> *   than to despair.*

> *When we return to*
> *   really trust in God,*
> *   there will no*
> *   longer be room*
> *   in our soul for*
> *   fear.*

Keep your hope alive. Acknowledge to yourself that you have an invisible, supernatural means of support. Once you can grasp this, then this imperative becomes logical—"Fear not." It is illogical to have anxiety. There is an option—obedience to God's command. It keeps hope alive.

FEAR NOT!